BLUDSO'S
BBQ COOKBOOK

**A FAMILY AFFAIR IN
SMOKE AND SOUL**

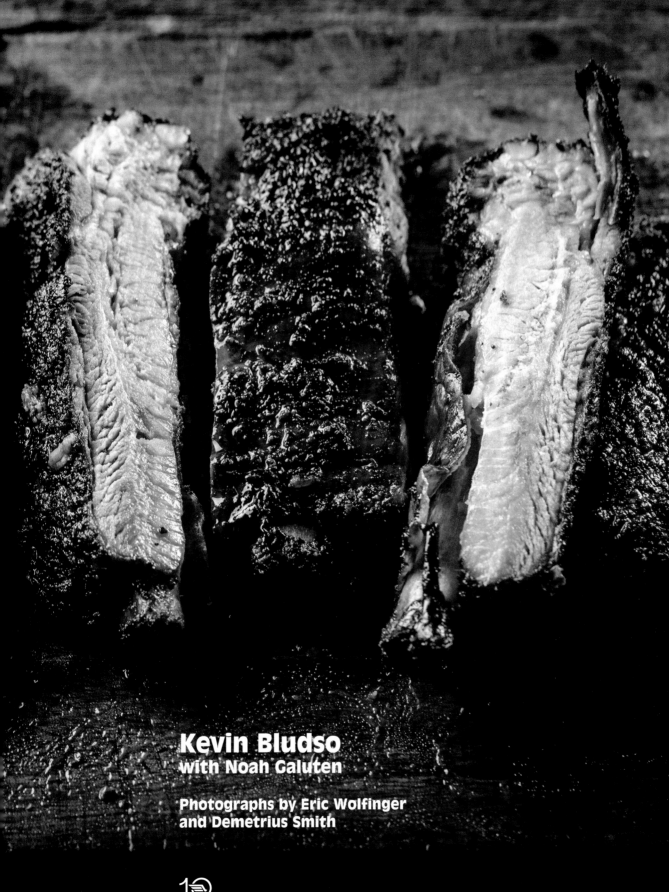

Kevin Bludso
with Noah Galuten

**Photographs by Eric Wolfinger
and Demetrius Smith**

TEN SPEED PRESS
California | New York

Contents

Introduction

I was born and raised in Compton, California, with a police officer father and a Black Panther–supporter mother. Every summer to stay out of trouble, I went to Corsicana, Texas, to work at my granny's illegal, bootleg BBQ stand.

I always just say that I'm so lucky to live the life I've lived. To be from Compton, to be born and raised with people like Dre and them in the city, in the concrete jungle, but then on the flip side to be able to be in the country every summer, to walk around barefoot, and go crawfishing and all that. Getting to grow up in both California and Texas gave me a whole different outlook than if I had just been raised in one place, and that's something I've been able to carry throughout my life. I just really think everything happens for a reason. Now I look back, and I've opened BBQ restaurants all over the world, I've gotten rave reviews from legends such as Jonathan Gold, I've hosted TV shows, I'm a two-time winner of the Steve Harvey Neighborhood Awards for Best Barbecue Place in America, and now I get to chill out and live in the country in Texas.

In this book, I want to teach you how to kick back, have fun, and make some good-ass BBQ. Then I also want to show you how I get down in the kitchen, too, cooking up way more than just BBQ. But for me this isn't just a cookbook. I also want to tell a story. I want to tell you about the family history, how we started, how we came to this, and a few of the things I've learned in my fifty-five years.

Shit Talking, Cooking, and Partying Lessons with Willie Mae Fields

I call her my granny, but Willie Mae Fields was really my daddy's auntie. She's the one who taught me how to BBQ. I swore up and down to her that I'd never go into the restaurant business. But Granny always said, "You're gonna have to own your own business because you're too much of an asshole to work for anybody else."

That first summer I went to Texas to stay with Granny, I was eight years old. I'll always remember that ride in her '74 gold, four-door Lincoln Continental. I was in the car with her, Aunt Alice, and Mr. Fred. (I still have no idea who Mr. Fred was. I don't even think he was family!) They were just partying, drinking, and driving, blues all in the car. The cooler was full of hog headcheese and sandwiches, and I was like, "What the fuck did I get myself into?"

Then in the house was Granny's crazy-ass husband, Johnny B., who was shell-shocked from the Korean War. So she'd say, "You want to stay here with this crazy motherfucker or you want to work with me in the morning?"

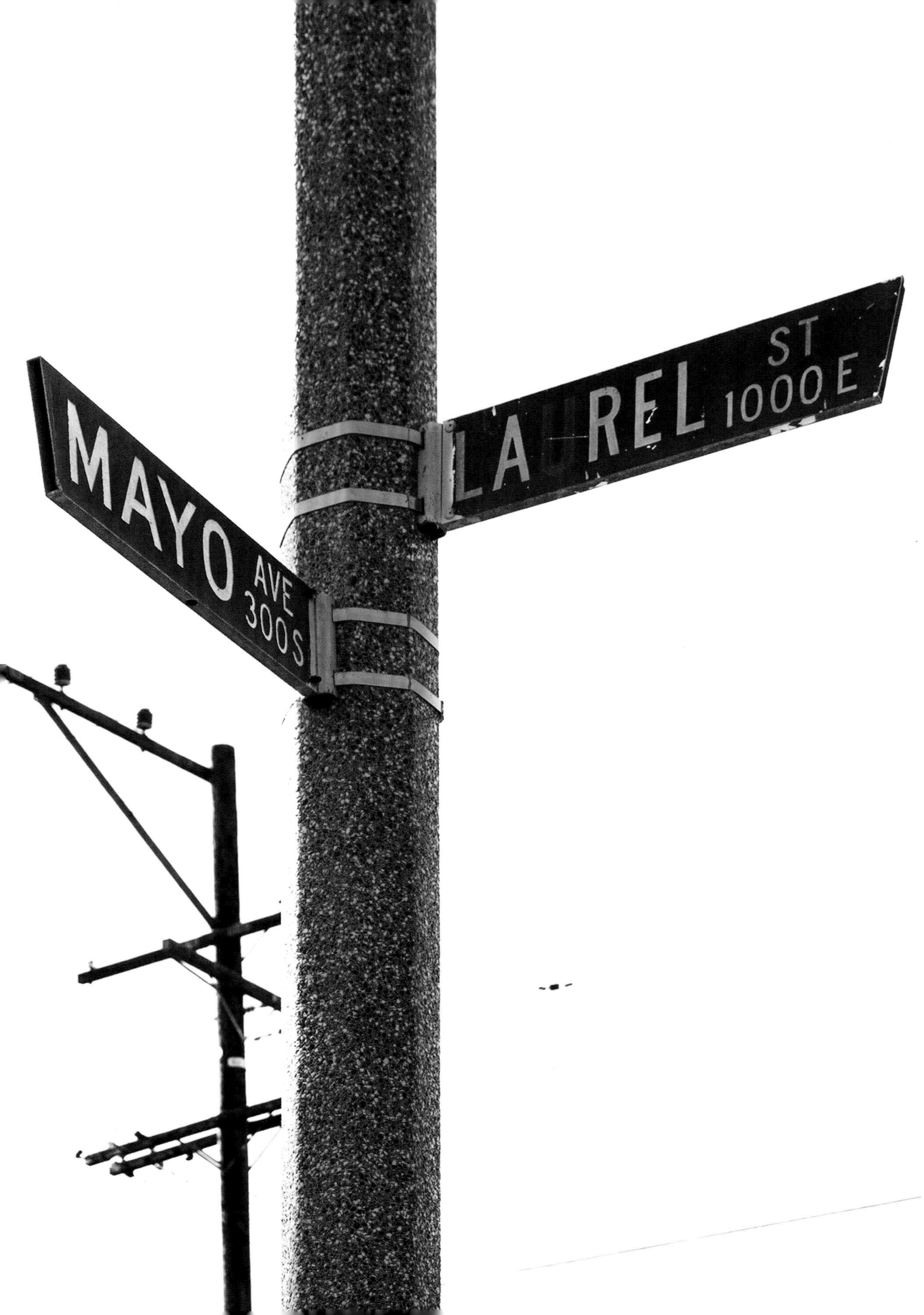
MAYO AVE 300S
LA REL ST 1000 E

So I started working with her, getting up at six o'clock in the morning and going to her illegal BBQ restaurant on the weekends, with gambling going on, with no permits or health department or anything. She called it Little Rascals, and I watched her work that stand with Aunt Jean and Aunt Alice. It was just the three of them running this restaurant so incredibly. And all they did was cuss out each other all day. As a kid I'm watching this shit, like "Wow." I wasn't used to sitting there with somebody cooking, telling a story, talking shit, laughing, playing the music all loud. I wasn't used to that, and that's what made it better. You see, my parents were young. They were still working, still humping, so when I would go out to Texas, it was something special. I was hooked right away, and I went back every summer.

Granny did so much for so many people. She put people up, fed people. She was a legend in Corsicana. She was ninety-five years old when she died. Something like fifteen thousand people lined the streets of the town for her funeral procession. Everybody knew Willie Mae Fields. But don't get me wrong, Granny was a hustler too. She ran her little businesses in the back — her after-hours club, some other little red-light shit. No matter what, Granny didn't believe in being broke.

She also had a small juke joint next to her house where she could probably fit fifty people at a time, selling BBQ, Crown Royal, Schlitz Malt Liquor, gin, and whatever else. She called it The Halfway House. The juke joint was really long, kind of like a house on one side where you've got the kitchen and all that. At one end was this tiny waiting room that had a little speakeasy door so she could look through it and make sure you weren't the law. After she'd let you in, you'd walk through the kitchen, where it was hot as hell. Past that there was a bar area with a couple of rooms off to the side in case you wanted to do some . . . other stuff. She had AC in all the rooms and in the bar, but it was all window units. Wasn't no central air. But everybody would party. The back was wide open and had a jukebox, though she would have bands in there sometimes — blues bands and stuff like that.

But shit, she wouldn't let me drink with her until I was, like, fifteen or sixteen, and even then it was just a beer or something. But I loved being out there in Texas with her. She taught me cooking, but she also taught me work ethic. She'd be up all night cooking a brisket — and having a cocktail — until two o'clock in the morning, but she'd still get up at six no matter what; and I'd have to get up with her. "You don't work, you don't eat," she'd say. We'd be smoking brisket, cooking collards, the whole thing. I still cook my greens the same way Granny cooked hers. I cook my brisket the same way. Eventually, I was the only other person she trusted to cook a brisket.

Granny also taught me the value of family. When my father or my grandmother — my dad's mom — would come down from LA, that was huge. Granny couldn't wait to show them a good time. She would prep food for a whole week. I'm talking, like, a hundred pounds of chitlins. She would just prep these massive amounts of food for the whole time that people were there. She and my grandmother loved each other to death, but they couldn't get along for more than five minutes. My grandmother would drive all the way out from LA just to argue with Granny. There was so much love, and sometimes they showed it by talking shit with each other.

Opposite, clockwise from top: Granny's mixed-use property — her house with her club, restaurant, and hotel next door in Corsicana, Texas; Granny always rose with me; I loved Granny's smile.

Clockwise from top: Family first; Pops; and Moms.

But talking shit was a big part of our family. I was Granny's baby, and she still always used to talk about my big nose. She'd say, "God wanted you to have a big nose so you could smell the bullshit." Some people trip on what they can't really change. In my family you couldn't grow up with a damn complex, because they talk about everything. They talk about each other's kids, each other's wives, each other's husbands, *everything*. Some of my best jokes come from me being in Texas with my granny, just watching the family clown and talk shit. It goes on to this day. My uncle still calls just so we can cuss each other out and laugh about it.

When Granny was growing up in the 1920s, her mom was working for someone on the other side of town — somewhere close to Corsicana, I'm not exactly sure where — so as a kid Granny went along to work with her. Granny started playing with this other kid named Bill, and they developed a friendship at a time when Black and white weren't supposed to be friends. They were five or six — little kids — and they had a friendship that went all the way until Granny passed away at ninety-five. Bill didn't live another year after she died. They were real close. That taught tolerance too. She'd say, "Bill has some good-ass racism jokes." But then she'd tell me, "You don't need to get mad; just flip it around!" They would sit around and just, as grown-ass people, crack jokes on each other. He'd have the nerve to be cracking Black jokes — well, they didn't call them Black jokes, but you know what I mean — and he'd tell one, sitting right next to me and be like, "You get that one?" And then his laugh would just make *me* laugh. But my granny loved him so much, and I loved him so much. They made it so that I didn't give a fuck if it was a racist joke or whatever, as long as it was from the heart and it was for comedy. There's a difference if you're saying shit and it's from hate. If it comes from hate, it's not a joke. But Granny taught me that there's humor in everything. Certain things are serious. There's no doubt about it. Certain shit is serious as hell. But you've got to find some humor. Just like you find the pain and you deal with it, you've got to find the humor in everything too.

At Granny's funeral, Bill came up and he couldn't talk. Our family, Unc and everybody, they came up and held him so he could speak. He loved us so much and loved Granny so much. He could barely talk. He just said, "No more jokes," and everybody knew what that meant. There wasn't going to be any fun anymore. Then he just kept saying, "She was my friend . . . she was my sister . . . she was my friend." They were *real* friends. People say, "Oh she lived to ninety-five, she lived a good life." And yeah, she did, but that doesn't make it easier for the people she left behind. I had that woman in my life for nearly fifty years, and I thank God for that.

The Family

Like I said, my moms, Jean Bludso, was a Black Panther supporter, and my pops, David Bludso, was LAPD, so you can imagine how that went. My mom's views were a lot more militant on a lot of shit. My mother's seen a lot of shit. My mother has seen *her* mother murdered. I know a lot about my mom's side, but there's a lot I don't know, too, because my mom's gonna carry a lot of that shit to the grave.

She was born in '47. She was nine or ten when her mom was killed. She got rushed out into the night by her uncles. I had actually always thought that my grandmother, my mom's mom, got killed in Texarkana. But I just recently found out that she was killed in Dallas at the Bluebird Café, where she was a waitress and a cook. From what I hear, it was a white lady who thought her husband was messing around with my grandma. He wasn't. Grandma was just getting off a sixteen-hour shift and a white lady came in and shot her. Then some other shit went down within forty-eight hours — there was another murder that was committed by somebody on Granny's side — so they had to scoot out of town. Never had a funeral for Grandma or nothing like that because they had to get out. Back in those days, if a white person got killed, they were gonna come looking for your whole family. It's still crazy to think about. That's my history. I've seen pictures of Grandma, and she was just such a beautiful woman. Somebody cheated me out of the opportunity of meeting her. My mother would ask me sometimes, "Do you think it's just Willie Mae that drew you to Texas?" And I say no. I think it's the ghosts. It's everything. I'd tell her, "I know your mother's got a whole lot to do with it. I know she's inside of me too."

But that was it. After that all went down, my mom had to leave town and the family got split. Some of them stayed in Texas, and she headed for LA because my Uncle Kaiser, Aunt Belle, and Uncle Sam were out here.

Then my mother became a legend in the projects in LA. Her family became one of the most-known gang families in Watts. My mom always made sure we stayed away from that shit, but she was hardcore in the goddamn projects. My father always tells this story; he says, "Man, your mama was so fucking crazy, because when some of these motherfuckers tried to jump me after a party in the projects, Jean had two switchblades on her, she pulled the motherfuckers out, and she had about three guys backed up and scared to come out of the motherfucking corner." Then my daddy's friend Skip would say, "I was there," and my daddy would laugh and say, "You was?! Because you sure didn't do shit!" My daddy would tell us, "If you ever call your momma's family on some shit, it better be some shit, because those motherfuckers were killers."

But like I said, she always made sure that we weren't a part of that. Somebody shot at my Uncle Carl once, so I brought over some of my guns — that's back when I was a corrections officer. I was just hanging out in the back, playing video games in Bellflower. Then my Uncle James came over. That's my mother's oldest brother. He's deceased now. And I just remember he didn't know I was there, and I could hear him talking. He said to somebody, "What do you wanna do? Motherfuckers can't be shooting at the family

Opposite, clockwise from top left: Auntie Helen doing her thing on the grill; 322 — Mom's house, good food and good memories; Always good times in The Blue Room; Uncle Kaiser holding court on the pit; Compton royalty, Mayor Emma Sharif and Mama Bludso; Uncle Kaiser giving BBQ classes to Cousin Alan back in the day.

like this. What's the plan? We need a legit plan to take care of this." I remember I listened to this and then I just popped out and said, "What's up, Uncle James?" And then he just went off. He grabbed me and he slammed me. He said, "What the fuck are you doing here?" I was, like, twenty-one, and he slapped me and he said, "Get the fuck out of here." I was so upset. I didn't understand. Why would Uncle James do that to me?

He came to my house later on that night and apologized. Then he said, "Some people in this family don't have nothin' to look forward to. This is not where you come from. You're different. Carl and them? They're fuckups. You ain't a fuckup. Don't you never let nobody get you into some shit like this. Never. Motherfuckers are about to get killed. I expect so much more out of you. Carl never should have even called you to bring him shit over here. Can you imagine what your mom would do if she knew you were here?"

I never forgot that. That's why I always say there's no such thing as peer pressure in the neighborhood. Because if there's peer pressure, you're just a weak motherfucker if somebody can make you do something you don't want to do. Nobody can make you join a gang. If you're doing that, that's what you want to do. It's the influence in your life. None of my siblings, none of my daddy's kids, has ever been arrested.

So like I said, my mother's family was legendary in Watts, but there's so much more to them. There were great cooks on my mom's side of the family who were a huge influence on my cooking. It wasn't just Granny who influenced me. There were lots of great grillers in my mom's family. My cousin Tony makes these great little BBQ riblets. My Uncle Kaiser — my mother's uncle — was an early BBQ teacher for my family. He lived on the west side of Compton, and he had this huge backyard. I think my mother and all of them learned BBQ from Uncle Kaiser. This guy looked like goddamn Frank Sinatra, but he talked like James from *Good Times*. He was a legend on my mom's side. Then there's my Aunt Beulah, who kind of took the place of my mom's mother when my grandmother was killed. She ran a candy store in the projects that was legendary and sold the stuff from her back door. She had an assortment of candies, potato chips, and chili cheese Fritos, and she'd make these damn Kool-Aid pops called icebergs. I'd get dropped off there to get babysat, and Aunt Beulah would say, "You damn curly haired motherfucker, you already had one of those icebergs. Don't be trying to hang out in the damn kitchen!" I'd always try to sneak something, and she'd say, "You can have one piece and go sit your ass down."

But my mom is what started it all for me. I was her number-one tester. My mother could BBQ better than my father, that's for sure. And that was always a big deal because Pops would put on some ribs, and Mom always had some extra backup ribs going because she said Daddy was gonna fuck his up.

My mom and dad got divorced when I was, like, six, but don't get me wrong, Pops was still around in my life. My pops has seen a lot of shit too. He was a Black LAPD officer when there weren't a lot of Black police officers. He was a Texas boy who was also from Watts, but he had to do things a different

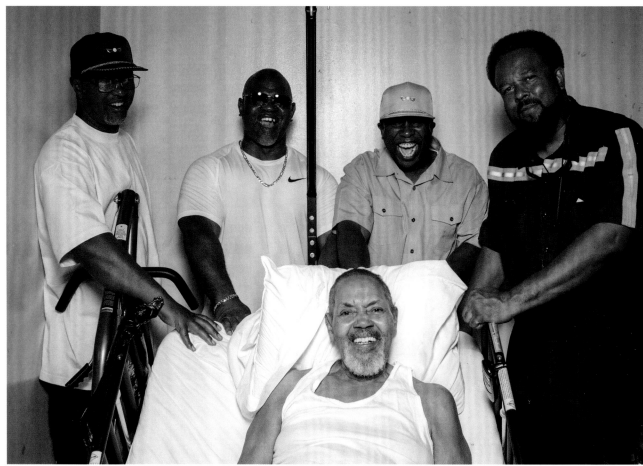

way from my mother's family. He was a cop, but he never kissed ass or nothing like that. My daddy is a prime example of a good cop. Like I always say, I support good cops, I don't support bad cops. Just like I support good protestors, but I don't support bad protestors. People hate the police until they need the police. But I hate bad police. They're criminals. They're fucking criminals. My father went thirty-five years and never had to shoot nobody. People sometimes say that it's the training that will stop bad police. But to me, it doesn't even start with training; it starts with background. Who are these people? The biggest thing about police is that there are a lot of cops who are racist. There are a lot of cops who were bullied when they were younger, and there are a lot of cops who never made the football team and never got over it. My daddy was one of the good ones.

I'm just now learning more about my dad's side because of research for this book. His family moved from Texas to Bakersfield, California, when he was three years old. "Yeah, we lived in a tent for a minute," he told me. "[Aunt] Mary Lou burned it down. Shoot, it's been a minute. Mary Lou used to cuss out airplanes and shit. But if you needed her in a fight, she was there. I call her ass, Geronimo." Not long after that, they moved to Watts.

He and my mom got together when they were just kids, and Mom was thirteen when she had my brother. They were together for about ten years. There were eight brothers and sisters but only three that are from my mom; the others are siblings from my daddy. Eight total but only six are left now. I'm my mom's youngest. We stayed in the projects at first — the Jordan Downs housing projects in Watts, Los Angeles. Daddy started working for UPS and then, in 1968, he became a cop. It was even in the paper. My mom helped him big-time with the police test and everything. Not long after that, we got the house in Compton.

When I was growing up in Compton, there was this little old white lady, Ms. Lee, who lived across from the street from us. She would start drinking that goddamn red-top vodka — that's the cheapest shit — and everyone called it that because you could see that little red top sticking out from her back pocket. She'd drink and then she'd start talking. She'd be in the middle of Compton calling us "niggers" — right across the street from our house. But my mom taught me a lesson on that too. My mom was militant, like I said, but even she'd be like, "Go over and kick her ass? Why am I gonna kick her ass? I could beat the shit out of Ms. Lee if I had to, but that ain't gonna get me shit. I don't want no easy wins." She taught me that Ms. Lee's shit was just ignorance, and there's nothing you can do about that. And all you do by going after her is make the situation worse. So Ms. Lee would be out there calling us all kinds of names, and my mom would just let it go. But then the next day, Ms. Lee would sit out there sober, just guilty as a motherfucker, waiting on me to come out. My mom would say, "Ms. Lee has been out there watering the grass for an hour, waiting on you to come outside, Kevin." So I'd go out and Ms. Lee would say, "Hey Kevin, can you take my trash cans out?" It'd be four days before trash day, and I'd be like, "Yeah, Ms. Lee." Then she'd give me, like, thirty, forty dollars for taking out one trash can. Then I'd come back inside and my mother would always say, "Boy, give me twenty dollars of that guilt money."

Above: My dad always served the community.

Opposite, top: The Doc and James Carthon (Pip). *Opposite, bottom:* There comes a time when the sons have to take care of the fathers. Bracy, Norm, James, and G.

But like my mom said, Ms. Lee was coming from ignorance, not hate. So you've always got to remember that too. Ignorance is what it is. Hate, to me, sometimes has to be matched with hate. That's when the Compton in me comes out on a lot of shit. If you try to get at me with hate, I'm gonna get back at your ass with hate. But I was taught, if you're an ignorant mother-fucker and I stoop to your level, then I'm just as ignorant as you.

Bludso's BBQ

My mother always said, "Go to college and get a degree so you can make decisions," which I did. After playing football at the mighty Dominguez High School, I went to play at Bishop College in Dallas, Texas. I still didn't want to go into the restaurant business, but I started catering at the dorms to make some extra money. Like Granny said, "You need a legal hustle." She would always stress *legal*. Some people get *hustle* fucked up as something negative or breaking the law. But she said legal. In life, there might be a time you need a job, a time that's slow and you need extra money. So my legal hustle back then was catering. I was in college selling chicken dinners, not even realizing that I was doing exactly what she said. It wasn't even in my mind that I was doing that, but there I was making money by cooking and DJing, doing the two things that I love: food and music.

Even then, I didn't think food would be a career for me. So after college, I went on to work for the California Department of Corrections. I sometimes think about one day when I showed up late for work. I might have been twenty-three or twenty-four years old. I used to get really depressed on Sunday nights because I had to work on Monday. So I showed up late one Monday, and Officer Kelly said, "Bludso don't like Mondays." Then Officer Frisco said, "Shit, you better get used to it. Bludso got another thirty years of Mondays." And I said to myself, "Oh my God." I didn't know what was going to happen, but I knew right then that this wasn't gonna be it for me. A few years later, I went to working paroles, and there was a lot of shit that I just couldn't keep my mouth shut on. So I ended up getting terminated, which wasn't my plan. But in the long run, it was the best thing for me. Years later, one of my training officers came to Bludso's BBQ and said, "Damn, Bludso, all this time I thought you were crazy as hell when you got fired, but now I see you had a plan." And I said, "No, I really didn't!"

The truth is, when I lost my job, it got tough. I had no plan, and I had a family on the way. But I fell back on my legal hustle, like Granny taught me. I started catering and DJing and, before long, I was making more money from that than I had been at the Department of Corrections. I started work-ing with this lady, Lulu, who hired me to help her out with the BBQ at her restaurant. It was slow to start, of course, and I remember at the end of the day she always took the ribs that were left over in the warmer and put them in a ziplock bag to sell again. Those ribs had been in a warmer all day; then the next day, when I saw her warming them back up, I said to myself, "When I open up my own place, it's gonna be tough at first, but I'm not gonna give nobody no old-ass ribs. Because that person coming in for the first time is gonna say this food ain't shit." She had this banquet hall, and when I'd see

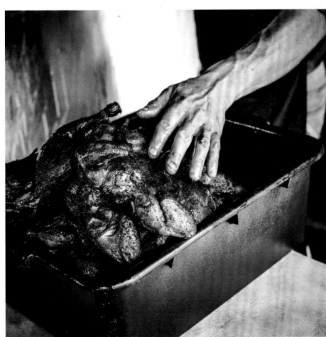

her cleaning up, she'd take a chicken off a plate and put it in a bag to reuse it at another catering event. She said to me, "You've got a lot to learn about catering." So I said, "No I don't. Not like the way you do it."

I learned so many lessons back then. One time my mom got me a catering job for the post office for one hundred twenty people. This was my first big job, and I fucked it up. I was late, the food was cold, and I was just totally overwhelmed because I was doing the whole thing for all those people on a little grill in my apartment. My mom was pissed. But I learned from that. I learned that not all money is good money. I shouldn't have taken that job because I didn't have the setup to do it right. So I told myself never to take on a big job like that until I'm ready. But the catering kept growing. I got a settlement from the corrections job and used that check to buy my first smoker. Then this building came up for rent in Compton on Long Beach Boulevard, and I took it. Nobody knew I did it. I didn't even tell my wife at the time, Monique. It was a big gamble because I really wasn't making much money. I don't even know how I was paying the rent. I had that building, paying rent for eight months before we opened up, making ends meet by selling dinners out on Rosecrans and Long Beach Boulevard.

Then in February 2008, I opened Bludso's BBQ. We were so lucky that it happened during the time of foodies and food TV. It was a time when Yelp and Chowhound were exploding. But my goal was to be just as good as the other places in LA. I wanted to be as good as Philip's and Woody's. I never had the thought of trying to put anybody out of business or anything like that. My mentality was straightforward — I know I can BBQ, I know I'm gonna have some good food, and I think I can make some money off of this. Monique remembers when I was working on all my recipes. She said, "I thought it was so good, but then you said it wasn't right, and you knew there was this taste you were looking for." Everybody was telling me "you gotta do breakfast, you gotta do hamburgers" and so on and so on. So I remember I called Granny, and she said, "All you gotta do is get known for your BBQ. There's already somebody doing burgers. There's already some-body doing breakfast. There isn't that much BBQ. Be known for your BBQ."

But back then people weren't coming to Compton from all over to try BBQ, and that first year started kind of mellow. Every day during those first few months, I would check Chowhound and Yelp and we had no reviews. So I went on Chowhound under a fake name and wrote, "Have you guys ever tried Bludso's BBQ? It's pretty good." And then this Chowhound regular and food blogger named Tony Chen — who hates it when I try to give him credit — jumped in and wrote, "Hey, who are you? Shut up, don't give away my place." He was clowning, but then he said that Bludso's is amazing and has got the best rib tips and so on. And just off of him posting that, people from all over started trying the BBQ. Then Bludso's just really started to grow. Not long after that, the great Jonathan Gold came in and gave us a rave review in *LA Weekly*, and that helped us a lot too. Food was getting so big back then and everybody wanted the story. We started getting all kinds of press and appearances on the radio. It was crazy.

Opposite, bottom, near left: My Cousin Cookie was there from Day One.

When we started, I was, maybe, doing ten racks of ribs a day. Then by the Fourth of July that next summer, I was up to doing seventy-five racks in a day. The numbers kept on growing, and when we hit our peak, we were doing two hundred racks of ribs on a regular Friday or Saturday. On our busiest holiday, we were doing something like one thousand racks in a day, selling them out of a twelve-hundred-square-foot restaurant. We were doing about one thousand smoked turkeys and eight hundred fried turkeys on Thanksgiving.

Let me tell you this; like Granny always said, I was too much of an asshole to work for anybody else. But working for yourself is the hardest job in the world. People see me now and they say, "Oh, I wanna kick it like you kick it." Well motherfucker, can you go eight years with just two or three days off that whole time? People don't realize that with BBQ, even if you're closed one day, you still gotta work that day. You still gotta season the meat, prep it out, put on the brisket for tomorrow. I aged myself about twenty years opening Bludso's. It was no sleep in those days. If I could get four hours every once in a while, I'd be like "cool." There were days when I had a line out the door, and I would cook the food, run the register, make the plate, hand it out, and then take the next customer. But to see it start from a takeout stand selling ten racks a day to what it's become now? To have multiple restaurants in Los Angeles, a restaurant in Australia, TV shows, awards, accolades, and all that — it's amazing. I knew I was trying to make something special, but there was no way to expect where it got to. But even now, I still feel like, with the team I have, we're nowhere near the top of the mountain.

Then, in 2016, after Bludso's Hollywood was already a huge success, I was still down in Compton working all the time. The building was falling apart, and I was talking to James Starr — Big Game James — my business partner, and he knew I was at my end. We were talking about trying to remodel Compton and all that, and he just asked me, "What do you want to do?" He was almost crying. He could see it in me. He said, "If something happened to you, we're all fucked. What do you want to do? Are you done?" I didn't know I was done at the time, but I was done. My health was bad, I was stressed out, and I didn't want to be done . . . but I was. I just thought that what we did in Compton was legendary. I mean, it still is. But closing the Compton location was the best decision for me at the time. I'm not one of those types of people who's got to work all the time. That's another lesson. Granny worked for years because that's what she wanted to do. But I don't want to be like that. I don't want to work for sixty-five years straight and then have five or ten more years to live. I don't believe in that. Mind you, I still work, and I still love to work. But not those twenty-hour days, seven days a week for months and months. But going on the road, shooting a TV show, training some new pitmasters — and then getting to come back to Texas and chill out and watch my Cowboys? That's alright.

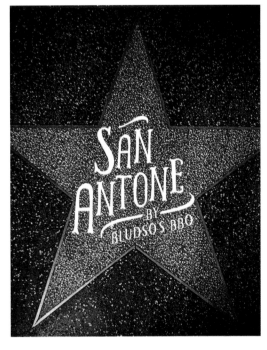

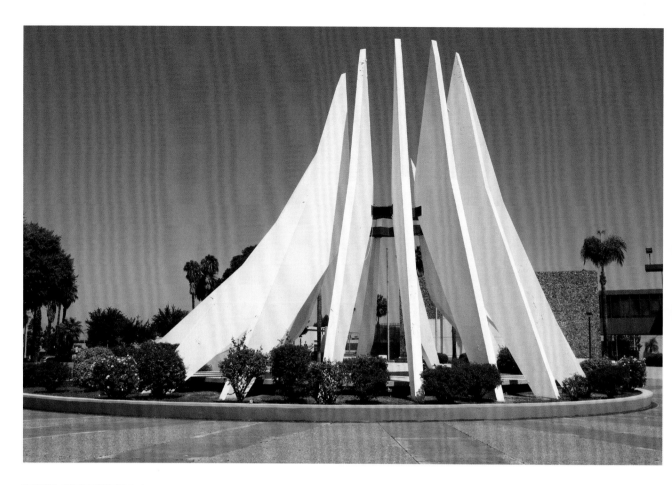

What Everybody Has Wrong about Compton

Bludso's BBQ helped break down so many barriers that kept people from coming to Compton. They thought that Compton was what they heard on the TV or radio news, and they soon learned that it was nothing like that. I always talk about when we had that shooting out front in 2009. A guy got killed right across the street, and we brought in some customers and locked the door. One white lady was hysterical. And I just grabbed her and held her, and she was saying, "Oh my God" and this and that. And I told her, "I'm so sorry. I've never seen anything like this before." And for some reason, that just calmed her down. I said I'd never seen anybody get shot before. I hadn't. She said that in her mind this was every day in Compton. And I told her it's not. I was born and raised in Compton, and it was the first time I'd seen somebody get shot. I'd seen scenes but never anyone get killed. *I* wanted to be hysterical. People get it twisted, because it's really not like that.

That's why I get so mad about this documentary I saw about the streets of Compton. There's a voice-over that says, "We walked into Dominguez, and we're stepping over bodies. . . ." That's a damn lie. You know what I'm saying? Who lives that way? Who would allow their kid to live that way? Why are you portraying something like that when it was nothing like that? I mean, if you're a gangbanger, it's out there. But we never experienced no shit like that. That's why I have problems with *Boyz n the Hood*. That is such unrealistic bullshit. People say that's the legend? The legend of a dead body rotting on a street corner and nobody doing anything about it? Do you know that's portraying you as a fucking cannibal? You're used to that shit? Oh, motherfucker, you're getting shot at, but you're walking down the street wanting to scratch a Lotto ticket? Or the biggest thing, when you get chased, you never break up. You never separate from each other. Why would you leave your best friend if people are chasing after you? Oh, you're getting shot at but you want to drink milk and scratch Lotto tickets and take a piss. That is so stupid. It's making us look like we're cannibals and we live like that, and we don't.

I remember a friend of mine from college. He was from Chicago. Now that motherfucker was from the ghetto. And he came out to Compton one time when we were juniors and said, "Man, I don't never want to hear nobody say Compton is no ghetto. Man, they've got *sprawling* front and back yards." I always remember that. Because we went to his house one time and I said, "Goddamn, this is so fucked up out here. The mailman just goes and dumps the mail on the corner and lets everyone sort it out." That's when I said I'm not from no ghetto. The thing is, people depended on the Compton Bludso's for so much more than food. We helped so many kids through poverty. We helped so many kids go to college. I would pay people's electric bills. I kept so many people's lights on. I kept so many people's cars from getting repossessed. If you came into Bludso's and you didn't have money, you were still gonna get fed. I was gonna take care of you. And that's what I want to say to you too. That's where your blessings come from. If someone is trying to get one over on you, then you figure that out for the long run. But I swear, the times we helped somebody out once,

98 percent of the time they came back and paid — even the homeless. I'd tell them, "You know this time I'll give you a chopped beef sandwich, but don't make this no motherfucking habit."

On the negative point, we also paid for too many funerals. Like when a little girl got killed in her house, we bought her a casket. It's not so much something we had to do for the community as it was just in us. And when I was at that little girl's funeral and the little casket that we paid for was brought out, I just had to leave. I couldn't do it. But my whole thing was, I don't give to be blessed. I'm blessed so I give. I just think sometimes you might have problems, but your blessings will come bigger by having a heart.

The Past and the Future

Running a business is tough. I had to miss a lot of my kids' games and recitals to get to a certain point in my career. But your kids are the reason you work one hundred fifty hours a week. Mine are the reason why I am the proudest father around. I'm about to have my third college graduate and hopefully two doctors to go along with a brilliant, amazing performer. My kids are everything. I used to wear hundred-dollar tennis shoes until I had my first child. I haven't worn a hundred-dollar pair since. Kids are supposed to make your priorities change. It's not about you anymore. Even building my dream was not about *my* dream; it was about a dream and a legacy for them. My whole thing is to make them proud. I want to make them as proud of me as I am of them. I want them to do 100 percent better than I did. My three kids are the major stars of my life.

And since family is everything to me, that's why it's been so amazing to learn more about my own family history after all these years. What's crazy is, I ended up connecting with my mom's side of the family that stayed in Texas after everything went down — the Griffins — because of Facebook. A family member saw me on TV and messaged me, "I'm an aspiring chef, and I think we might be cousins." This is in, like, 2017. It all connected, and a few of them came over one time. Shit, one of them damn near wanted to swab me for DNA to make sure. The coldest part is they were all here and Cousin Dee said, "I'm gonna call my Auntie Annie. She's eighty-eight." So she called her and said, "Hey, what's going on?" And then she said, "I've got a surprise for you." Then Auntie Annie said, "What?" and Dee said, "I'm gonna put you on with him." So I took the phone and said, "Hi, Ms. Annie. I'm Kevin."

"Oh okay," Ms. Annie said. "I don't think I rightfully know you."

"I'm Jean's son," I said.

"Jean? I don't know if I know a Jean."

Then I said, "I'm Daisy's grandson," and all you heard was the phone do a *thwack*. Then you heard a rustle and this other cousin got on the phone and Dee took the phone back and said, "We found Daisy's grandson." The woman on the other side of the phone just said, "Oh my God."

Then Annie got back on the phone. She was crying and said, "I always wanted to know what happened to them kids." So at first I'm thinking she was talking about us. Then I realized she was talking about my mother and her siblings. They were the kids. So she went down the line naming all my mother's siblings, but she didn't say my mother's name. Instead she said the name Red. "Who's Red?" I said, and then I found out that was my mom. I just remember I called my momma and said, "Who's Red?" And she just paused and then said, "Who you been talking to?"

The Bludso Family Tree

I could have easily just written this cookbook all on my own, but that wouldn't have been fair because my family is a part of me. They taught me how to cook and also how to treat people. I will always want to share my family with the world — all of their truth, their lessons, and their comedy. It wasn't until I was older and would start telling stories about them that I realized how unique and special they really are. I've got so many grannies and aunties and uncles who aren't even really that, but we call them that because it's a sign of respect. Some friends are too close to just call *friends*. The people I grew up with in Compton are more than just friends. James Starr and Noah Galuten and Jimmy Weathersbee are more than *just* friends.

Like Granny said, if she loves you, you're family. That's what family is to me, and it's just like that with BBQ too. It's more than just food. It's a family function. In my family, 99.9 percent of the best experiences were around food — hanging out in the kitchen, cooking, eating, and talking. That's why I'm just so proud to introduce my family and our food to you.

Below: My mother's mother, my grandfather, my mother and her siblings. That's my moms all the way on the left. Grandmama Daisy, holding Uncle Bub, my Grandfather Hubert holding my Auntie Aileen, my Auntie Mary, Cousin Alan, and my Uncle Willie.

Page 26, top center: My grandmother holding my brother David, rest in peace, Debra, and my daddy holding me. *Middle left:* Me, back in the day *Middle right:* My mom at work *Bottom:* The family. I learned BBQ from both sides of my family. Uncle Kaiser was a great teacher of culinary.

Granny

Dallas

Deb

Moms

Iman

Aliyah

CJ

Ashleigh

Jordan

Hayley

Liam

Pops

Chris

Clay

Kevin

Nikki

Chalil

Chyna

Aryus

Monique

Amir

What's in My Kitchen?

Here are the things that I always keep around when I'm cooking at home. If you have them on hand, it'll be so easy to go shopping just for meat, and you'll be able to make most of the stuff in this book. Many of these recipes have a lot of the same things in them — and I always grab extra of these ingredients because they're what I use the most. Just make sure your pantry is tight. And have it way more organized than my pantry.

CAYENNE PEPPER

Cayenne pepper, baby. If it ain't hot, it ain't me. Some people are very intimidated by cayenne pepper until they learn how to use it. Cayenne is good for adding heat, but it's also a flavor enhancer. The right amount of cayenne brings out every flavor in your dish. I'd use it in place of MSG powder any day. I love the Fiesta brand, if I can find it.

CHICKEN BOUILLON POWDER

Many recipes in this book call for chicken bouillon powder. It's used both for its flavor and for building flavors. And it's got so much salt in it that you'll notice the recipes don't even need to call for any regular salt. But because of the salt amount, you must be careful when you use it. Knorr makes an excellent chicken bouillon powder.

HOT SAUCE

When it comes to hot sauce, everybody — wherever they're from — has their version of what they like. Tabasco, Frank's RedHot, Louisiana; I don't care as long as it's good. I like a hot-hot sauce, but I don't like it overly hot. I like something flavorful. My personal favorite is probably Texas Pete Hotter Hot Sauce. But if I'm traveling in another state, I love seeing different hot sauces. I collect those.

KITCHEN BOUQUET

If you looked in the cabinet of any kitchen I went to growing up, you'd find Kitchen Bouquet. I always just call it a darkener, but it's more than that. Originally it was meant to just kind of speed up a dark roux, but I stand by it. I use it in a number of the gravies and roux in this book.

SEASONING SALT

Salt is just salt. So why not add a little flavor to your salt? I use just a little sprinkle of seasoning salt in my greens, in my BBQ rubs, and in the breading for frying pork chops or chicken. If I had to pick, I'd rather have seasoning salt than just regular salt. Fiesta and Lawry's both make great ones.

SMOKED HAM HOCKS

Shit, I'd put a smoked ham hock in my cornbread if I could. I think it's just some of the best-flavored meat in the world. It gives good flavor to a broth, it cooks off well, and it's nice and fatty. Plus, even when you use a hock to flavor a broth, the meat still keeps its great flavor after having been boiling in the water for a couple of hours. It's amazing for beans and greens. It also freezes really well, so grab some packs when you go to the store and keep extras in the freezer. I hope people don't get too hip to hocks, or the price is gonna start going up like it did with the damn oxtails.

SPICY PEPPERS/CHILES

It really depends on what you're cooking, but I always have hot peppers and chiles in my kitchen. I love banana peppers for my beans and my greens, but they can be hard to find sometimes. So I started using serrano chiles, which have a very good flavor that blends really well but is still spicy enough. Then if I want it even hotter, I'll add a habanero to kick up the heat a little bit. I like to put one into my pinto beans (see page 129), which flavors the whole pot. I like to eat the whole habanero that's in there, but I'm probably the only one who does.

I always keep dried peppers around, too, like the guajillos or New Mexico chiles that I use in my Red Chili Burrito (page 117). They give a little heat but also great flavor. Then there are the pickled jalapeños that I have on hand to eat with fried chicken.

HOW TO BBQ— KEV'S WAY

The first thing about BBQ is, don't take it too seriously. You're cooking outside, so more than likely it's gonna be a beautiful day. You're chilling. You got some good meat on there. BBQ is supposed to be fun. BBQ is supposed to be positive. Even if you can't cook worth shit, it's just people coming together to have a good time. Always keep that in mind. I don't want the BBQ in this book to be like some kind of damn algebra class.

Learn the craft and always respect the game. Even if you really want to learn BBQ to become the backyard king, just remember it's still fun. You're not gonna go to jail for learning how to make BBQ. BBQ is a party. Have fun with this shit. Who doesn't want to hang out and come try what you're doing? When you're cooking at home, if you like it and your friends like it, you're good. If you're trying to go into business, then yeah, you've gotta hone your craft. But shit, if you've got a line out the door, keep doing what you're doing. Just take the time to really learn the craft, and have people that you trust to give you unbiased opinions and who are gonna keep it one hundred.

Just Don't Make Bad BBQ

There are a lot of ways to make BBQ, but like I always say, just don't make bad BBQ. These are some things I've learned over the years to make BBQ the way I like it. So I'm going to give you some tips for what kind of smoker to look for and how to treat it right.

What Kind of BBQ Pit Should You Buy?

Don't get caught up on how much the pit costs. I've tasted incredible stuff cooked on cheaper pits, and I've tasted horrible stuff from expensive pits. I'm gonna show you how to use a classic charcoal grill to make BBQ, too, but if you're buying a smoker, the main thing is it has to be an offset smoker. That means that your firebox (where the wood and charcoal burn) is in a separate place from the racks where the meat goes. The offset smoker allows you to get to your wood and your charcoal without disturbing your product. It also keeps the smoker at a more consistent indirect heat. Both of these things will make for better BBQ.

Then make sure it's a tuned pit. This means that it cooks within about 10 degrees from one side to the other. It should also have at least a couple of air vents that you can use to control the temperature — usually one at the top of the stack (the flue is the control valve inside of the stack) and a second vent on the side of the firebox. It's pretty simple when you think about it. The more air you let in, the more the fire will flare up. The less you let in, the more you'll choke the fire out. Try to find a smoker with a drain on it. A brisket has a lot of fat, so when you smoke it for twelve hours, a lot of the fat is going to render out and drain off into your pit. That is delicious fat, and you want to be able to reserve it and add to your BBQ sauce.

As for the size of your pit, that really depends on what you're trying to do. But once you're barbecuing, you may as well have some space to fit a few things on there. The best-tasting BBQ comes from whole logs of wood instead of wood chunks (don't even bother with wood chips if you want to make real BBQ). Having a firebox big enough to fit whole logs is the dream. But don't worry about it if you can fit only chunks, that'll work too.

At the end of the day, if you're a serious smoker, don't get a pit until you can afford one that's high quality and won't warp. If you want to do catering, find the one that you love and then get one that's a size up from that.

How to Season Your Pit

With a brand-new pit, the first thing you have to do is season it; you have to smoke it out or your meat will taste like a fucking robot.

Start off by spraying your pit with vegetable oil or bacon grease. Grease the whole inside from top to bottom — the walls, the doors, the racks, everything. You've gotta get that metal flavor out of it. The more you cook on your pit, the better your BBQ will taste.

Next you want to give it a hard smoke. I like to smoke a brand-new pit for at least ten hours before I put any meat on it. I'll smoke it at around 250°F with some oak and some pecan. You'll see that the racks, the doors, and the walls will turn dark. Just keep on smoking at 250°F, adding wood as you go.

Learn Your Pit

The most important thing is to learn your pit. Every pit is a little different, and once you start cooking and learning how your pit works, the better your BBQ is going to turn out and the more fun you're going to have cooking on it. Take the time to practice on your pit and get the hang of it before you start smoking a big-ass, expensive brisket. Figure out how much charcoal it takes to get you to the temperature you want. Learn your hot spots and your cold spots. Every pit is different, and the right temperature comes with practice. It's always good to put an oven thermometer in there to make sure the thermometer on your pit matches up and is showing you the right temperature.

The Biscuit Test

BBQ pits have hot and cold spots. It's important to know where they are so you can put the right meats in the right places. The most accurate way to know where they are is to lay a bunch of oven thermometers throughout the whole smoker and then fire it up and see what they say.

But the easiest way is the biscuit test. Get your pit to 250°F and then open up a can of biscuits and put them all over your pit. Then, to learn where the hot spots are, watch to see which biscuits cook the quickest.

What about Wood?

The size of the wood that you use depends on the size of your pit. Like I've already said, if you can fit logs, that's great. And if not, chunks are fine. But don't ever use chips; they're for grilling, not smoking. But this all comes with learning your pit.

You also want to try to find wood that is dry. Most BBQ wood sold in hardware stores will be pretty good. Just be careful if you're using a commercial wood supplier. Ask if the wood has been aged before you buy it. You should also look up pictures of the wood online to see what it's supposed to look like. There are scammers at every level, and if you don't know what the wood is supposed to look like, you can be at their mercy.

How to Light Your Pit

The BBQ recipes in this book will give you specifics on which wood to use, the temperature, and how long to smoke. But here are my basic tips for getting your smoke going.

The first thing to do when you light a fire is start with a charcoal base. Lump charcoal is better than charcoal briquettes because it's just burned-down wood and that's it. It has the best flavor, and it burns cleaner and longer than briquettes, which have all sorts of chemicals and filler in them. All lump charcoals are different, so read the bag. It should tell you the easiest way to light it. I prefer to stack mine like a pyramid. And never use lighter fluid. Use something clean-burning, like hay or kindling. When you're lighting the charcoal, remember that it heats from within, not out to the end — so give it the time to really ignite. Don't think that because you don't see flames that it isn't lit. Let the charcoal burn until it's ashed over. That means it's gray, like your granny's hair, but still has a little flame. That's how you know you're ready to add your wood.

Spread the charcoal into an even layer and then lay the wood logs or chunks over the top. If they are logs, they can overlap a little; if they are chunks, just lay them right on top of the charcoal. But really it all depends on the size of your firebox and what will fit. The goal is to get a good, consistent smoke, not a raging fire.

The next important thing to remember is you want to let your wood burn off the bitter smoke before you add your meat. This takes five to ten minutes. A good test is just to look at the smoke. At the beginning, when the smoke is bitter, it's darker; then it'll lighten up and you can put on your meat. Once the smoke is going well, you will barely see any rising out of the stack. Nearly all of it will stay inside the pit. It's not supposed to be barreling out of the stack like the Number 10 coming in from North Carolina.

Tending Your Fire

Always monitor your firebox and your temperature because you don't want to oversmoke. Most of the flavor from the wood comes at the beginning. As you get to the end, you're mostly using charcoal to keep an even heat. A brisket might take ten, twelve, or even sixteen hours to cook, but it can't take on all that smoke the whole time. That's why when you're smoking a brisket, you can start wrapping it after it's got a good bark on it. Then you're just cooking and not oversmoking.

Now like I said, everybody has their own preference on how they treat the firebox, but this is mine. When the first log or wood chunks are almost burned out and your heat is dropping below the target temperature or temperature range at which you want to be cooking, you need to add more fuel. You don't want the wood or the coals to burn out totally, as you never want to have to catch that fire again. Then on the longer smokes (like brisket and pork shoulder), when you're done with the wood flavor, you just go with charcoal the rest of the way.

You're regulating your heat two ways: with wood and charcoal, and with the firebox vent and your stack (which is also called the flue). When you add a fresh log or wood chunks or some charcoal to your pit, the temperature will spike. So you want to close the door of the firebox and close the airflow on the stack a little (but never all the way) to bring the temperature down. A consistent temperature is one of the most important things in BBQ. Every BBQ recipe in this book will have either a temperature range you want to stay within or a target temperature you want to stay as close to as you can. Just remember, wood and charcoal both affect the temperature, but the wood is what really gives you that smoke flavor.

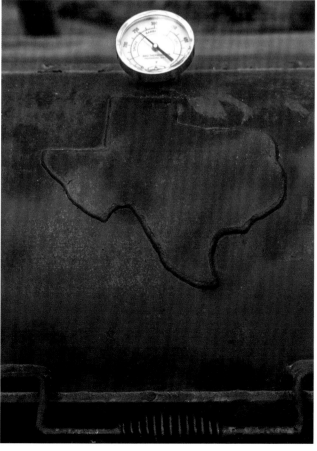

Troubleshooting

If your heat spikes way up, the first thing you want to do is open up the door of the pit and let that temperature come down. When you open the pit, you'll be keeping your meat from burning, and you can look to see if there are any flames coming out of the firebox. If the pit is just running hot and hasn't caught fire, wait until the temperature drops back down, then close the door to the pit. After that, close up the side vents and top flue a little more to see if you can get the temperature back to where you want it.

If the pit really catches fire, the first thing you have to do is take out the meat and then close up all the vents and the stack and smother that fire. Just because the pit is burning up doesn't mean your meat has to burn up. Don't fuck up dinner.

If the temperature is too low, adjust it by adding a bit more charcoal right into the firebox. (You never want your flame to go out, so you should always be able to add charcoal and wood straight in the firebox.) Don't add a ton — just a little at a time and keep an eye on it. This is all part of learning your pit.

There Are No Set Times on BBQ

In each recipe, I give you a window of how long it usually takes to cook the item, but don't worry about the time too much. I've cooked briskets the same way so many times, and sometimes they just take longer. BBQ is done when it's done. It can be the weather, it can be the wood, and it can be the meat. Think about all the times you've cooked a steak and sometimes it just comes out different. Sometimes you're just at the mercy of the butcher.

Get Your Confidence up with Chicken

I always say the best thing to start with is chicken. If you're using your pit for the first time, once you've got it all seasoned (see page 36) and ready to go, try it out with chicken. It cooks quickly, and you'll really be able to taste the smoke on it. Start out with classic BBQ chicken (see page 89) and then go from there. Plus, if you don't like how it turns out on the first try, chicken is less expensive than a rack of ribs or a brisket.

How to Clean Your Pit

Never, never, never, never, apply any type of chemical cleaning product to the inside of your smoker. If you use chemicals, your BBQ will taste wrong forever.

The only thing you ever clean are the racks, and most of the time you're just brushing them. If you keep up with your racks, you'll never need to use chemicals to clean them. What matters with your racks is that the holes don't close up. If they close, the smoke can't get through. So after you've been making BBQ for a while, it's good to brush off the buildup on your racks. You can even wash them with soap and water in the sink if you need to. Just make sure there's no soap left on them before they go back into your pit.

Don't forget to clean out the bottom of your pit every time you finish using it. Just drain the grease and then scoop out all the bits of meat and rub that fall to the bottom of the pit and throw them out. If you don't drain your grease, you'll be wondering why you have maggots in your rub. Especially during the summer — after cleaning, hit it with a water hose or the heat will really make the grease start to rot. Too much grease can also flame up. I'm telling you that one with a smile because I'm speaking from experience.

Also, never keep any cleaning supplies in spray bottles by your pit or you might accidentally spray your ribs with them. I've done that too.

SLAP IT, FLIP IT, RUB IT DOWN

The rub is the base of building your flavors. It is what starts you off making great BBQ. These are great bases, and you can take them and run with them. Or you can take a rub and add to it. For example, the base of a great BBQ pork rub is salt and sugar, so you can just build your rub from there. The rub is where the crust of your meat comes from. If somebody pulls a piece right off the top of that rib and tastes it, it's your rub that's being tasted—that's your crust, so you want it to be good. Then the sauce is the accent that sets it off. The rub, the smoke, and the sauce all have to work together.

Speaking of which, I hate when someone disrespects a rub by not putting it on right, because we've got some really good-ass rubs. So make sure you always dry off your meat with a paper or kitchen towel before you pat on a rub. If the meat is wet, the rub will get all lumpy and caked on, and it won't form a good crust.

Dry rubs will keep indefinitely if you store them in a tightly sealed jar or other airtight container in the pantry.

Bludso's Brisket Rub

Brisket rub is just garlic salt and pepper. That's all you need. Now once again, you should do what the fuck you wanna do. That said, I can't stand when people put sugar on brisket. I just think brisket is such a good-tasting meat, like prime rib. What do you do to prime rib? Salt and pepper and *maybe* a little rosemary. You don't have to do too much. At Bludso's, we use prime briskets, too, and if you smoke them the right way, that smoke, salt, and pepper are just perfect. I've always hated sweetness on my beef. Save your sugar for your pork and your cocktails, like Hennessy on the Rocks (page 244).

MAKES 2¼ CUPS

1¼ cups garlic salt

1 cup coarsely ground black pepper

In a medium bowl, combine the garlic salt and pepper and mix thoroughly. Store in an airtight container at room temperature.

Bludso's Steak Rub

Try this rub with some garlic butter on Grilled Steak (page 113) and you'll be really happy. I also use this rub to season my oxtails. Now, if you know me well, you know I don't like to put sweet on beef, so just understand that the sugar in this rub is not for sweetness but to bring out the flavors of all the spices and make them pop.

MAKES ABOUT 2 CUPS

¾ cup seasoning salt

½ cup ground black pepper

¼ cup granulated sugar

¼ cup ground cumin

¼ cup granulated garlic

1 tablespoon granulated onion

½ teaspoon cayenne pepper

In a medium bowl, combine all the ingredients and mix thoroughly. Store in an airtight container at room temperature.

Bludso's Pork Rub

My granny used just salt and pepper on her ribs, but I wanted to come up with something a little different for mine. I love sweetness on my pork, but I wanted it to be savory. That's why I use both dark and light sugars—I want sweetness, but I don't want overpowering sweetness. I want a little heat on there too. We use this rub on our pork ribs and our pork shoulder, and it gives the crust a nice dark color.

MAKES ABOUT 4½ CUPS

1 cup seasoning salt

½ cup packed dark brown sugar

½ cup granulated sugar

½ cup coarsely ground black pepper

½ cup finely ground black pepper

½ cup ground cumin

½ cup dark chili powder

¼ cup granulated onion

¼ cup granulated garlic

1 tablespoon cayenne pepper

In a large bowl, combine all the ingredients and mix thoroughly. Store in an airtight container at room temperature.

Bludso's Lamb Rub

Between visiting so many different restaurants and growing up with my mom's influence from her heritage and background, I really grew to love lamb. Now I could tell you more about the specifics on my mom's background, but she likes to keep that stuff a secret. Just know that I wanted a mix of Indian, Mediterranean, and Moroccan spices on the lamb, and I wanted something that was going to enhance the flavor of the meat without overpowering it.

We use this rub for our Smoked Lamb Leg (page 99), but it will work on nearly any lamb dish you like.

MAKES ABOUT 1¼ CUPS

In a small bowl, combine all the ingredients and mix thoroughly. Store in an airtight container at room temperature.

¼ cup seasoning salt

3 tablespoons sweet paprika

3 tablespoons granulated sugar

2 tablespoons ground cumin

2 tablespoons ground coriander

2 tablespoons ground cardamom

2 tablespoons ground cinnamon

2 teaspoons ground cloves

2 teaspoons ground nutmeg

2 teaspoons cayenne pepper

Bludso's Chicken Rub

This is my twist on the seasoning for pollo asado–Mexican grilled chicken–but done as a dry rub for such Bludso classics as BBQ chicken (see page 89) and Smoked Chicken Wings (page 111).

MAKES A GENEROUS 3 CUPS

1¼ cups seasoning salt

⅓ cup granulated sugar

⅓ cup ground cumin

⅓ cup ground black pepper

¼ cup granulated garlic

¼ cup granulated onion

2 tablespoons dark chili powder

2 tablespoons smoked paprika

1 tablespoon ground oregano

1 tablespoon cayenne pepper

1½ teaspoons ground turmeric

In a large bowl, combine all the ingredients and mix thoroughly. Store in an airtight container at room temperature.

Fish-Fry Seasoning

As much as folks in my family like BBQ, pretty much every Friday night–on both sides of the family–we were frying fish. But it's funny, as no matter which side of the family we're talking about, almost the exact same little hook-up is used to fry fish. It's not that fancy or complicated or anything, but I think it's just incredible.

MAKES ABOUT 4½ CUPS

3 cups yellow cornmeal

½ cup seasoning salt

½ cup ground black pepper

¼ cup granulated garlic

¼ cup granulated onion

2 teaspoons cayenne pepper

In a large bowl, combine all the ingredients and mix thoroughly. Store in an airtight container at room temperature for up to 6 months.

Bludso's BBQ Sauce

You always want to be able to eat your BBQ without the sauce—that's the test. Your sauce is not a lifesaver to rescue bad meat. BBQ sauce is supposed to be a condiment to complement great meat. So why not have a good-ass sauce with some good-ass meat? I prefer a spicy sauce, and this is a quick one. If you don't want that heat, then just back up off the cayenne and the red pepper flakes. This sauce is great with brisket, ribs, pulled pork sandwiches, and all that. Some people might prefer a thinner or thicker sauce, but this is a nice base to go off of to find your own recipe. If you are in a hurry, you can just strain and serve at room temperature instead of putting in the fridge overnight.

MAKES ABOUT 3½ CUPS

6 tablespoons salted butter

1 cup finely chopped yellow onion

2 tablespoons finely chopped garlic

2 teaspoons yellow mustard

1½ tablespoons cayenne pepper

½ teaspoon seasoning salt

2 teaspoons mustard powder

½ cup packed dark brown sugar

2 cups ketchup

⅔ cup cider vinegar

⅓ cup Worcestershire sauce

4 teaspoons red pepper flakes

2 tablespoons liquid smoke

Cooking Equipment: Heavy, medium saucepan

In a heavy, medium saucepan over medium heat, melt the butter. Add the onion and garlic and stir. Once they start sizzling, add the yellow mustard, cayenne, and seasoning salt and stir to mix well. Next, add the mustard powder and brown sugar and stir to mix. Then add the ketchup, vinegar, and Worcestershire and, again, stir to mix. Finally, add the red pepper flakes and liquid smoke and stir until all of the ingredients are well mixed. Turn the heat to low and allow the sauce to cook at just below a simmer for 10 minutes to blend the flavors.

Remove the sauce from the heat and let cool to room temperature, then cover and refrigerate overnight. The next day, strain the sauce through a fine-mesh sieve. Transfer to an airtight container and store in the refrigerator for up to 2 weeks.

When ready to serve the sauce, reheat gently on the stove top; do not let it boil or you could ruin it.

Granny's Gravy

When I first opened up Bludso's in Compton, I tried to make it as authentic as I could to respect the work that Granny had put in. If you love something and you've got good taste, then you've got to do it that way to show people how good it is. But when it came to Granny's "sauce," everyone was like, "What is that?" In Texas, they understand these thinner dipping sauces, but back then in Compton, they just didn't get it. So try this out to put a different twist on your brisket or your ribs. It's really more of a dipping sauce or a basting sauce than a traditional BBQ sauce, and I just love it. And if you like spicy, you can heat this up with some red pepper flakes and a little more cayenne.

This gravy is the reason to always keep your smoked drippings from cooking a brisket. And make sure that you stir up the gravy when you serve it, since there is a lot of fat that will sit at the top.

MAKES ABOUT 4½ CUPS

In a medium bowl, combine the brown sugar, paprika, bouillon powder, black pepper, chili powder, cumin, and cayenne and stir to mix well. Set this seasoning mixture aside until you need it.

In a heavy, medium saucepan over medium heat, melt the butter. Add the onion and garlic and stir. Once they start sizzling, add the ketchup and vinegar and stir to mix well. Next, add the Worcestershire, steak sauce, and hot sauce and stir to mix. Finally, stir in the seasoning mixture, then add the drippings and liquid smoke and stir well.

Turn the heat to low and allow the gravy to simmer, stirring occasionally, for 20 minutes to blend the flavors. Transfer to an airtight container and store in the refrigerator for up to 2 weeks.

When ready to serve the gravy, reheat gently on the stove top; do not let it boil or you could ruin it.

¼ cup packed dark brown sugar

1 tablespoon sweet paprika

1 tablespoon beef bouillon powder

2 teaspoons ground black pepper

2 teaspoons dark chili powder

1 teaspoon ground cumin

1 teaspoon cayenne pepper

½ cup salted butter

1 cup finely chopped yellow onion

6 garlic cloves, whole or chopped

¼ cup ketchup

¼ cup cider vinegar

3 tablespoons Worcestershire sauce

2 tablespoons steak sauce

2 teaspoons hot sauce

2 cups smoked brisket drippings

½ teaspoon liquid smoke

Cooking Equipment: Heavy, medium saucepan

OG
BBQ

What are you getting when you go into an OG BBQ restaurant? It may have loaded baked potatoes and all that, but you want brisket, pork spareribs, sausage, pork shoulder, rib tips, and beef short ribs. All the traditional offerings, which I have organized as such in this chapter. Shit, chicken is only borderline OG because a lot of places back in the day didn't even have chicken on the menu. As crazy as it is, I think sausage might be my favorite thing to try at a good OG BBQ spot.

Smoking on a Grill

Since not everybody has an offset smoker, I am also giving you a way to make some good BBQ on a regular charcoal grill. It's still more of a grill than a smoke — hotter than a smoke but colder than a direct grill. You can cook ribs, a whole chicken, chicken wings, rib tips, and sausage this way, but a whole brisket or pork shoulder is too long and too slow of a cook for a grill.

You'll need a standard charcoal grill (the bigger, the better) with a hinged grate on top that allows you easy access to the coals throughout the cook, and one or two charcoal baskets (depending on the size of your grill). You're going to be setting up the baskets all the way to one side of the grill and keeping some wood chunks smoking on top of the coals. The meat will be all the way on the other side of the grill to get as indirect a heat as possible. The idea is never to have any meat directly over the wood or charcoal.

When you cook this way, it goes a lot faster than a regular smoke, so you'll need to really keep an eye on it. A good pair of grill gloves is a big help, too, as you're still going to have to lift the grate to tend the coals and add wood.

How to Light Your Grill

First, review lump charcoal and charcoal briquettes in How to Light Your Pit (page 39), then light your charcoal according to the package directions, making sure the charcoal or charcoal baskets are pushed to one side of the grill. (If you're using a traditional grill such as a Weber, simply fill your charcoal baskets to the top — one basket for a small grill and two baskets for a large grill.) No matter what setup you use, try to create some type of medium-low offset heat, so that you don't have a flame directly below the meat. By keeping the heat source off to the side, you slow the cooking process and give the wood smoke a chance to penetrate.

Once the charcoal is covered with ash, lay three or so wood chunks on top (the types of wood will be specified in each recipe). Allow the wood to burn off for about 5 minutes, then put the grill grate on the grill. From here, you're ready to start grilling your meat according to the recipes.

Brisket

This is where I got my start—watching my granny be up all night cooking brisket when I was a little boy. You'd see this big-ass tough piece of meat, then you'd go to sleep and the next day everybody was talking about how good it was. Brisket was her favorite meat, and I felt like I got to be a part of it. Then when she got older, I was the only person who made brisket that she would eat. One of the highlights of my life was making her brisket whenever I'd go to see her. So I felt like brisket was something I had to master.

Now, if you can't make good brisket, you ain't doing no good BBQ. I still just like brisket with some baked beans (see page 191) and potato salad (see page 182). But brisket tacos, brisket hash, brisket sandwich—there's so much you can do with it. It's tough but it's delicate, and you make it soft as hell by the time you're through with it.

One 12- to 15-pound beef brisket

Yellow mustard for rubbing

About 1½ cups Bludso's Brisket Rub (page 48)

Wood: Oak and pecan

Temperature: 245° to 255°F

Rough Cook Time: 10 to 14 hours (It totally depends on the size of the brisket, but can take longer or shorter.)

Cooking Equipment: Smoker, instant-read thermometer (optional), butcher paper (optional)

Choosing and Prepping a Brisket

I like a whole brisket that weighs between 13 and 15 pounds. I would never go above 15 pounds, and I'd be really careful going under 12 pounds. When I'm smoking a brisket, I only use a whole brisket; never one that has been split up (like a brisket flat or a brisket point).

If it's your first few times cooking a brisket, I advise you to buy a brisket with as much fat as possible and to leave all the fat on. If it's competition BBQ, you need to trim the fat down a little bit. If you're already pretty good with brisket and it's just for the house, I'd leave all the fat on. God gave that fat so we wouldn't dry out the brisket. That means the more fat you're cutting off, the better chance you're gonna dry out the brisket—especially on the lean end. Unless it's some totally huge fat cap, just leave that whole thing on there.

Also, when you season that fat, the fat renders, and the salt gets into the meat. So the fat gives you room to season it hard too. The fat can take that salt. But while brisket can take salt, it can *really* take pepper—which is the classic taste of Texas BBQ.

Seasoning Your Brisket

You can season your brisket the same day you're going to smoke. When I'm cooking at home, I usually season it, then start up the pit and put the brisket on right when the pit is ready.

The first thing to do is dry off your brisket with a paper or kitchen towel. Next, take a little mustard and just give the brisket a nice, even layer all over. Make sure that mustard is rubbed in too. You don't want any clumps. You aren't even going to taste the mustard; it's just to help keep the rub on there and help out with developing a nice bark.

CONTINUED

Brisket, continued

Next, you want a lot of seasoning. But again, you don't want it to clump up; you just want a nice, even layer. I hate it when I get a brisket with clumps of seasoning on it, so please don't do that. Take your brisket rub and start out on the top of the brisket, going extra heavy on the fat cap. Rub that seasoning in to help it stick. Then flip the brisket and hit the bottom. The bottom never touches the table that you're seasoning on. When you're done, you should barely see the meat through the seasoning.

That's it. Just keep it ready until it's time to smoke. If you flip it back over, just make sure to cover up any bald spots on the brisket with some more rub.

Smoking Your Brisket

Follow the instructions in How to Light Your Pit (page 39), aiming for a temperature of 255°F. When the charcoal is ready, start with about eight oak chunks and let them burn off for 5 to 10 minutes.

Now load the brisket in the center of your pit, positioning it so the fat end is pointed toward the firebox. Then you're just keeping an eye on your temperature and your firebox but never opening the pit. The brisket needs that hard smoke for the first 3½ to 4 hours, so keep it steady with wood smoke, trying to time it out with adding the wood. Whenever the temperature starts to drop down to 245°F, add more charcoal or wood to the firebox. If it needs more wood, add about four chunks of oak, knowing that the temperature will spike each time.

Once you hit the 3-hour mark on your smoke, start blending in a pecan chunk with the oak. Then after the 4-hour mark, you can go to pecan and charcoal for another 2 to 4 hours, or until the brisket gets that nice bark that you're looking for.

If you are wrapping your brisket. We don't always wrap briskets cooked on a home smoker, but sometimes we do. If this is your first time smoking, it's a little Texas crutch that can help keep the meat from drying out. If you want to wrap it, you should do so between 6 and 8 hours into your smoke, after the brisket has a nice bark and is a deep mahogany color. If you're nervous about whether the time is right, you can double-check it with a thermometer. The middle of brisket should register about 170°F. After you've wrapped the brisket in butcher paper, put it back into the pit. Once it's wrapped, you can raise the heat to about 265°F and start cooking with just charcoal the whole rest of the way (or you can keep it in the 245° to 255°F range if you have the time). You don't need to use any more wood once the brisket is wrapped—just charcoal.

If you are not wrapping your brisket. After 6 hours, you are still going to go with straight charcoal the rest of the way, but if the brisket isn't wrapped, you will want to keep the pit between 245° and 255°F.

CONTINUED

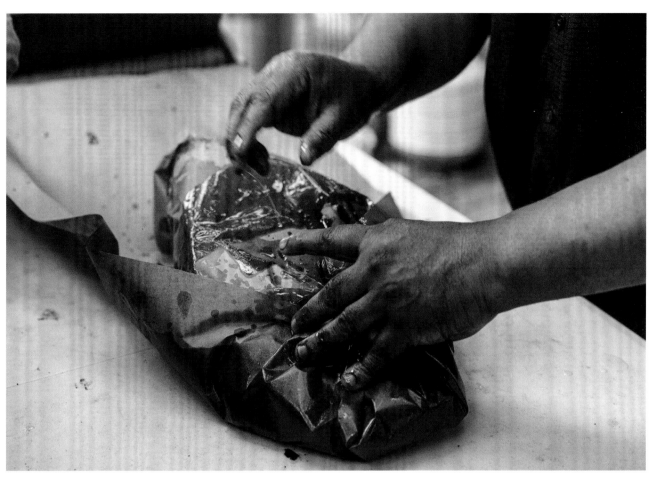

Brisket, continued

Now just keep maintaining that temperature. Once you hit the 10-hour mark, you can start checking on your brisket to see if it is done. You should be able to feel a soft, loose jiggle on it, even through the paper. It should feel as if all the fat has softened up and relaxed. You can also use a thermometer; the internal temperature should read 195°F. I've always just checked it by feel, but the cool thing is that the internal temperature and my feel test usually match up. If the temperature is right but the brisket doesn't *feel* right, keep cooking. The internal temperature is just a reference, not a rule.

Once the brisket has that feel, take it out of the pit and let it rest (in the wrapper, if you're wrapping) for at least 20 minutes or up to 1 hour. Then, if it's wrapped, open up the paper and let it breathe for another 20 minutes.

Carving Your Brisket

I like to use a serrated knife or a good, sharp carving knife for brisket. I cut down the center against the grain and then slice backward toward the tip of the lean end to get those best cuts (right where the lean and the fat meet each other). But if you cook the brisket right, the lean end should still be juicy as hell.

Once the brisket is cut, it has a horrible shelf life. If you're cutting, you should be eating. Cutting causes it to lose its color and dry up real quick. So if you aren't eating the whole thing right away, don't carve the whole thing. Instead, just carve the parts you want to eat right then. After that, you're better off saving it in the fridge and then cutting it cold and warming it. "Warm" is the main thing too. Don't heat it up too hot; it just needs to be warm.

Leftover brisket will keep, well wrapped, in the refrigerator for up to 1 week.

The "If You Get Drunk and Go to Bed" Method

Sometimes if I was a little late getting the brisket on the pit in the morning, and I've had a few cocktails and don't want to stay up late waiting for it, I'll use this method. After the brisket has been on for about 8 hours, I'll wrap it in aluminum foil, get the pit all the way up to 300°F, make sure the temperature is kind of sitting there stable, and then go to bed. The temperature will slowly drop throughout the night. When you get up in the morning, you can see how your brisket feels. It will sometimes still need a couple of hours, but this method is a way to get a little sleep and not take it too damn seriously.

Pork Spareribs

Brisket and pork ribs—they're like Bonnie and Clyde. People all over the world love ribs, so you'd better know how to do it right.

Ribs, like brisket, are a tough cut of meat, so while you're using that smoke for flavor, you're also using a low-and-slow temperature to tenderize the meat. If you don't take your time and smoke your ribs right, they'll be tougher than four motherfuckers from Watts.

One "4-and-down" rack pork spareribs (3½ to 4 pounds)

Yellow mustard for rubbing

Ground black pepper (optional)

About ½ cup Bludso's Pork Rub (page 50) per rack

Apple juice for spraying

Wood: Oak, pecan, hickory (optional), and apple

Temperature: 250° to 260°F

Rough Cook Time: 3 to 4½ hours (A St. Louis cut, for example, will be a little faster than a Compton Cut. But remember, BBQ is done when it's done.)

Cooking Equipment: Smoker, spray bottle

Choosing and Prepping Pork Spareribs

A St. Louis–cut rib is very popular. It's basically a sparerib slab that's trimmed all the way down into one neat little rectangle. With this recipe, one full rack will turn into a rack of ribs and some flap meat (some people call that flap the "skirt").

You can buy St. Louis–cut spareribs ready to go. You can definitely do that, but that's not how I like to do it at home. I like to start with a whole "4-and-down" sparerib rack. That means the weight of the rack is 4 pounds or less. I trim off the top bone (this is a rib tip, but it'll be kind of small to smoke for anything other than a little snack) and then I trim the flap off the back. I leave the rest of the meat on the rib. This leaves you with a bigger, meatier rib than you get with the St. Louis cut. In fact, when I showed this rib to Guy Fieri on *Diners, Drive-Ins and Dives,* I called it "The Compton Cut."

Dry off the rib rack with a paper or kitchen towel. Then lay it, meat-side up, on your cutting board with the narrow end of the slab pointing toward you. This next part sounds complicated, but it's actually really easy. Identify the rib tip on top; the rib-tip bone will come down 1 to 1½ inches from the top of the right side of your slab. Slide your knife (make sure it's a sharp knife) right under the bottom edge of the rib-tip bone. Then slide the knife from right to left, guiding it across that bone. The meat will tell you where it wants the knife to go. Once you get toward the end and the bone has disappeared, slide the knife upward until it has left the rib. You should now have one long rib tip and one trimmed sparerib slab.

Flip the rib slab over and find the lean flap meat hanging off the center of the back. Use your knife to cut that off. You can save that meat for things such as Spicy Maple Breakfast Sausage (page 207) if you want.

I don't trim the membrane on a pork rib. It's gonna be gone by the time you finish cooking it.

Seasoning Your Pork Spareribs

Spread a thin, even layer of mustard all over the ribs, rubbing it in well and making sure there are no clumps. Sometimes I also add additional black pepper to give a little more flavor, and you can do that too. Just add the black pepper first, before the pork rub. Season the back side lightly with

CONTINUED

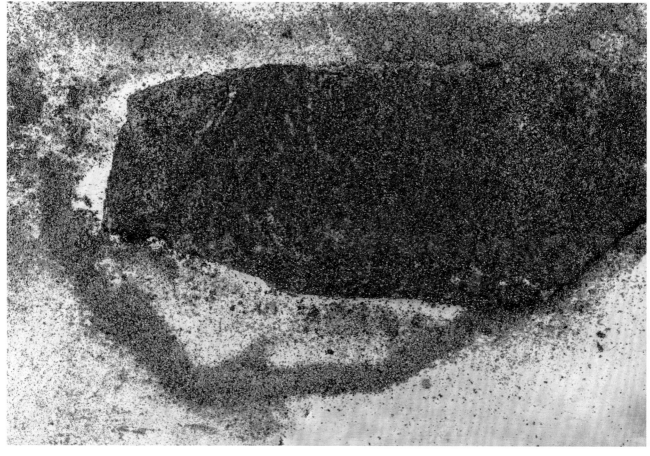

Pork Spareribs, continued

the pork rub and then go heavier on the meaty side. With pork rub, if it stays on top of the rib without chunking up, you're not using too much. Gently pat the rub so it sticks and then apply a second layer and pat it in. You want that nice crust on that rib.

Smoking Your Pork Spareribs

Follow the instructions in How to Light Your Pit (page 39), aiming for a temperature of 260°F. When the charcoal is ready, start with about 70 percent oak and 30 percent pecan. If you want to use hickory, too, you can go with about one-third each oak, pecan, and hickory. Let the wood burn off for about 5 minutes, then put the grill grate on the grill.

Now load the ribs, meaty-side up, into your pit and then watch your temperature. Every time the temperature dips down to 250°F, add a little more charcoal, and wood as needed. But on that first drop in temperature, add in a chunk of applewood with a little more of the other woods and some more charcoal. Apple can really darken your smoke, so you have to be careful. After about 2 hours, you can go pecan and charcoal the rest of the way.

Once the ribs have that reddish color and that crust is solid—after about 2 hours—start spraying them with apple juice. You want to spray enough juice so you see the moisture on the whole slab. The juice will revive the rub, which will start building up a nice crust. From then on, every time you open your pit to check on your ribs, you should be spraying them with juice.

When you think your ribs might be done, open the pit, give them a spray, and then pick up the slab at the center with a pair of tongs and look to see if it has a nice bend to it. If it bends and breaks, that's overcooked. If it's a rubbery bend, it's not done. It shouldn't have any bounce to it. Once you think it has a nice bend, feel the bone at the toughest part of a rib; it should feel like you could almost pull it out. It'll have some give to it when you try to twist it from that meat. Remember to keep spraying those ribs every time you check on them. When the ribs are ready, pull them off the pit and then let rest for 15 minutes before you cut into them.

Carving Your Pork Spareribs

I like to first cut lengthwise down through the middle and then off of each half. That first rib on the small end ain't shit, so when you start from the middle, you can really see how you did. When I cut, I like to have the slab with the bone/membrane side facing up so I can see the groove on the ribs and find the cut. The ribs curve down the back, which is hard to see when you're looking at them from the meatier side. Using a regular chef knife, slice down between those ribs in nice, clean cuts. If you're not going to eat the whole rack right away, keep any parts you aren't going to eat uncut.

Leftover pork ribs will keep, well wrapped, in the refrigerator for 5 to 7 days. Cut them while they're cold and then heat, covered with some plastic wrap, in the microwave just until warm.

CONTINUED

Pork Spareribs, continued

Grilled Pork Spareribs

Wood: Oak, pecan, hickory (optional), and apple

Temperature: Medium-low, indirect heat

Rough Cook Time: 1½ to 2 hours

Cooking Equipment: Charcoal grill, spray bottle, butcher paper or aluminum foil (optional)

Set up your grill as instructed in How to Light Your Grill (page 61). When the charcoal is ready, start with about 70 percent oak and 30 percent pecan. If you want to use hickory, too, you can go with about one-third each oak, pecan, and hickory. Let the wood burn off for about 5 minutes, then put the grill grate on the grill.

Place the seasoned ribs on the side of the grill away from the charcoal and wood and cover the grill, leaving the vent in the lid above the ribs open. Check the ribs, charcoal, and wood every 30 minutes or so, adding more wood chunks every time they have burned out. On the second load, you can add a chunk of applewood along with the other wood. You should also add more charcoal as needed.

Once the rub is set and the crust looks solid—after 1 hour or so—you can start spraying the ribs with apple juice every time you open the grill to check the meat and the fire.

If the color on your ribs is getting too dark, open the vent over the charcoal side of the grill (or rotate the lid so the opening is over the charcoal instead of the meat). If the color keeps getting darker and the ribs haven't finished cooking, go ahead and wrap the ribs with butcher paper or aluminum foil and put them back on the grill.

The ribs are done when you can feel tenderness and a little pull between the bones on the thickest part of the rib. They won't be quite as tender as slow-smoked ribs, but they shouldn't be tight either. Spray the ribs with apple juice just before they come off the grill, then let them rest for 10 minutes before carving as directed.

Sausages

Believe it or not, sausage is my favorite thing at a BBQ restaurant. Sausages don't take long to smoke, but you're still trying to go low and slow to get that smoke flavor and to keep the casings from splitting in the pit. And remember, the sausage you buy matters. The best smoke in the world won't fix a nasty-ass sausage. Make sure it's a raw sausage and not one that's already smoked; otherwise, you're not doing shit. Read the package if you aren't sure: it *has* to be raw. It's always good if you've got a butcher or somebody who makes one up that you like. I like a good all-beef sausage with a lot of fat that's not too skinny.

Truthfully, if you're smoking links, you probably have something else on the pit, too, so don't worry too much about the wood blend on these. Just cook them with whatever else you've got smoking, keeping the sausages in a cold spot of the smoker.

Raw sausage links

Wood: Oak or pecan (though you can use whatever you like)

Temperature: Around 230°F

Rough Cook Time: 1 to 3 hours for a slow, light smoke, depending on the thickness.

Cooking Equipment: Smoker

Smoking Your Sausages

Follow the instructions in How to Light Your Pit (page 39). When the charcoal is ready, add the oak or pecan chunks and let the wood burn off for 5 to 10 minutes. You're usually smoking sausages in a cold spot of your pit along with whatever else you're cooking, so you're targeting a smoke somewhere around 230°F. But a little higher is okay too.

Now load the sausages into your pit. Whatever else you are smoking will get the priority on the wood, the charcoal, and the temperature. Just monitor the sausages and don't let the fire get too hot or the casings will split. As long as the sausages are not sizzling from the heat, they are pretty durable on a smoke. They are ready when they are cooked through and have a nice smoke on them—anywhere from 1 to 3 hours, depending on the sausage size. Let them rest for about 5 minutes before slicing.

Slicing Your Sausages

I like my sausage thinly sliced and cut at an angle. But sometimes I also just like it whole, with a piece of white bread.

Leftover sausages will keep, well wrapped, in the refrigerator for 5 to 7 days.

Grilled Sausages

Set up your grill as instructed in How to Light Your Grill (page 61). Start with oak or pecan. But just as when I am smoking sausage, I usually grill sausages when I've got other stuff on there with them, so the type of wood you use isn't as important here, as long as it's something you like. Let the wood burn off for about 5 minutes, then put the grill grate on the grill.

Place the raw sausages on the side of the grill away from the charcoal and wood and cover the grill, leaving the vent in the lid above the sausages open. Check the sausages, charcoal, and wood after about 45 minutes. The most important thing is to keep your sausages on the coldest part of the grill. If the sausages get too hot, their casings can split. Your sausage is ready when it's cooked through and has a nice smoke on it. Slice as directed.

Wood: Oak or pecan (though you can use whatever you like)

Temperature: Medium-low, indirect heat

Rough Cook Time: About 1 hour

Cooking equipment: Charcoal grill

Pork Shoulder

Just like a brisket, a pork shoulder calls for long, slow cooking—and a lot of smoke. In fact, the cooking process is almost the same as for brisket. I love the way the dark meat on a pork shoulder takes on that smoke, and I love the red color it takes on too. Then the sugar in our rub really brings this all together. When that fat gets juicy and hooks up with that rub, it tastes like a pork shoulder pie or something.

My favorite way to eat a pork shoulder is as pulled pork—when it's pulled really thin and then piled high on some white bread with Bludso's BBQ Sauce (page 54).

Choosing and Prepping a Pork Shoulder

The good thing about a pork shoulder is that it's got a nice amount of fat on it. If you can find a shoulder with the skin still on the fat cap, that's even better to smoke. You want a lot of fat and some good marbling. I prefer shoulders that look like a ham bone.

Seasoning Your Pork Shoulder

Some people season a pork shoulder way in advance of smoking, but as with everything else in this book, when you're just cooking at home, you can season it and put it right in the pit when everything is ready.

Dry off your pork shoulder with a paper or kitchen towel. Spread a thin, even layer of mustard all over the shoulder, rubbing it in well and making sure there are no clumps. Next, give it a heavy layer of the pork rub and pat it in gently so it sticks. You can go really, really heavy on the rub on a shoulder. Then apply a second layer of the rub and pat it in.

Smoking Your Pork Shoulder

Follow the instructions in How to Light Your Pit (page 39), aiming for a temperature of 255°F. When the charcoal is ready, start right off with about four hickory chunks and one pecan chunk. Let the wood burn off for 5 to 10 minutes.

Now load the shoulder, fat-side up, into your pit and then watch your temperature. Any time it drops to 245°F, add more hickory and some charcoal. For the first 4 hours, it's mostly hickory with just a little bit of applewood mixed in. Then it's just pecan and charcoal for the next 1 to 2 hours.

When you've got a good color on your shoulder—5 to 6 hours in—you can wrap it with butcher paper and put it back into the pit. Once it is wrapped, you can go with just charcoal the rest of the way.

CONTINUED

One 8- to 10-pound bone-in pork shoulder

Yellow mustard for rubbing

About 1¼ cups Bludso's Pork Rub (page 50)

Wood: Hickory, pecan, and apple

Temperature: 245° to 255°F

Rough Cook Time: 8 to 12 hours (The bigger the pork shoulder, the longer the cook. But it could be longer or shorter.)

Cooking Equipment: Smoker, butcher paper (optional), instant-read thermometer (optional)

Pork Shoulder, continued

If you're not sure whether the time is right, you can double-check with a thermometer. The middle of the shoulder (not touching bone) should register 165°F. I don't always wrap pork shoulders, but if you're nervous about it coming out good, the paper will keep it nice and moist for you.

Once you hit the 9-hour mark, you can start checking on your shoulder to see if it is done. The best way to know if it is ready is to grab the bone. It should feel as if it wants to come out when you pull on it, but the meat should not be falling apart just yet. The outside of that meat will be real leathery too. Just remember, that bone can't come out if the shoulder isn't cooked.

If the shoulder is wrapped, you should still be able to feel the bone loosening up. Feel the bone when you first wrap the pork and then feel it again after a few hours, or when the internal temperature hits 200°F. But don't get too caught up on temperatures. Certain meats—sometimes it's not you—just act differently or need a longer cook. You want the meat to be loosened up and tender feeling but not be falling apart. When the shoulder is ready, take it out of the pit and let it rest (in the wrapper, if you're wrapped) for 20 minutes to 1 hour. Then if it's wrapped, open the paper and let it breathe for another 15 minutes.

Pulling Your Pork

Some people shred or chop their pork, but I like to pull mine by hand—lightly and not in chunks. It should almost be feathery. Only pull as much pork as you are going to eat; it's best kept whole and pulled off as needed.

Leftover pork shoulder will keep, well wrapped, in the refrigerator for 5 to 7 days.

Rib Tips

Rib tips are the most underrated cut of BBQ in the world. I love the really meaty ones that come off huge pigs. The ones you get off a regular rack of ribs are a little small. A lot of markets don't carry rib tips, so you might need to talk to a butcher and special order them. They are an excellent game-day or party food.

I'm old-school on rib tips and love smoking them with our brisket rub. Granny would just roll the rib tips in leftover brisket seasoning, which I think might be where I got the idea. It also makes them taste differently from the pork ribs. I think they're actually easier to smoke than a rib, too, because of all the extra collagen.

And just remember that dry flap meat on the end isn't worth shit. I keep it on during the smoke but I don't eat it. Throw that out or give it to your dog.

Choosing and Prepping Rib Tips

The bigger, the better when it comes to rib tips. You really want a big, meaty piece. Just keep in mind that the lean tail (flap) on a rib tip is basically a throwaway.

Seasoning Your Rib Tips

Dry off your rib tips with a paper or kitchen towel. Spread a thin, even layer of mustard all over the tips, rubbing it in well and making sure there are no clumps. Then add a layer of the brisket rub. It should be nowhere near as heavy as you would put on a brisket. Pork can't take pepper the same way that beef can. Just make sure the rub is even and covers well.

Smoking Your Rib Tips

Follow the instructions in How to Light Your Pit (page 39), aiming for a temperature of 260°F. You can really smoke these exactly the same way you do pork ribs, so smoking ribs and rib tips together works really well. When the charcoal is ready, start with about 70 percent oak and 30 percent pecan. If you want to use hickory, too, you can go with about one-third each oak, pecan, and hickory. Let the wood burn off for 5 to 10 minutes.

Now load the rib tips, meaty-side up, into your pit and then watch your temperature. Every time the temperature drops to 250°F, add a little more wood and charcoal. On that first drop in temperature, add a chunk of applewood with the other woods and some charcoal. Apple can really darken your smoke, so you have to be careful not to add too much. After about 2 hours, you can go pecan and charcoal the rest of the way.

CONTINUED

Rib tips, each about 2 pounds (the bigger, the better)

Yellow mustard for rubbing

About 1½ tablespoons Bludso's Brisket Rub (page 48) per tip

Apple juice for spraying

Wood: Oak, pecan, hickory (optional), and apple

Temperature: 250° to 260°F

Rough Cook Time: 2½ to 4 hours (The bigger the rib tip, the longer the cook. But always remember there are no set times on BBQ.)

Cooking Equipment: Smoker, spray bottle

Rib Tips, continued

Once the rib tips take on some color and the rub has started to form a crust—after about 2 hours—you can spray the rib tips with apple juice every time you open the pit to check on them or the fire.

You know rib tips are done when they start to have a little more looseness to them. They won't get as relaxed as a rack of ribs, but you'll feel some of that tightness ease up on them. Rib tips can sometimes take more than 4 hours, depending on the piece of meat. Spray them with apple juice just before they come out of the pit, then let rest for 10 to 20 minutes before carving them.

Carving Your Rib Tips

Start carving at the flap part and cut that whole tough end off and toss it—to your dog if you have one. Then cut backward toward the fat end—if you hit some bone or cartilage, it might just take a little extra muscle to get through it. I cut the tips into medallions about ¼ inch thick, but sometimes I'll cut them even thinner than that. If a rib tip is tender, you can really cut it however you like.

Leftover rib tips will keep, well wrapped, in the refrigerator for 5 to 7 days.

Grilled Rib Tips

Set up your grill as instructed in How to Light Your Grill (page 61). When the charcoal is ready, start with about 70 percent oak and 30 percent pecan. If you want to use hickory, too, you can go with about one-third each oak, pecan, and hickory. Let the wood burn off for about 5 minutes, then put the grill grate on the grill.

Place the seasoned rib tips on the side of the grill away from the charcoal and wood and cover the grill, leaving the vent in the lid above the tips open. Check the tips, charcoal, and wood every 30 minutes or so, adding more wood chunks every time they have burned out. On the second load, you can add a chunk of applewood with the other wood. You should also add more charcoal as needed.

Once the rub is set and the crust looks solid—after 1 hour or so—you can start spraying the rib tips with apple juice every time you open the grill to check them and the fire.

If the color on your rib tips is getting too dark, open the vent over the charcoal side of the grill (or rotate the lid so the opening is over the charcoal instead of the meat). If it keeps on getting darker and the tips haven't finished cooking, you can go ahead and wrap the tips with butcher paper or aluminum foil and put them back on the grill.

You know rib tips are done when they start to have a little more looseness to them. They won't get as relaxed as a rack of ribs, but you'll feel some of that tightness ease up on them. Spray the rib tips with apple juice just before they come off the grill, then let them rest for 10 minutes before carving as directed.

Wood: Oak, pecan, hickory (optional), and apple

Temperature: Medium-low, indirect heat

Rough Cook Time: 2 to 3 hours

Cooking equipment: Charcoal grill, spray bottle, butcher paper or aluminum foil (optional)

Beef Short Ribs

Short ribs are a Texas staple. They're just about the closest thing to cooking a brisket on the bone. In fact, you can smoke them the exact same way you smoke a brisket–they'll just be done a lot faster. Sometimes I wrap a short rib, and sometimes I don't. If it's been going perfectly the whole time and there is a nice amount of fat, you can just let it go. But if you get a little worried about it, you can wrap it once you've got a nice crust.

I don't know what first made me crave huge short ribs–being in Texas or watching Fred Flintstone. But either way, I love them.

Choosing and Prepping a Beef Short Rib Rack

You want that top fat and not too thick. You want marbling on the inside of the meat too. I like a three-bone rack that's 2 to 2½ inches thick. Some people take off the membrane, but I don't bother when I'm cooking at home. It'll cook off if you smoke the ribs the right way. If you want to remove it, get a flathead screwdriver and try to slide that just under the membrane on the back side of the rack. Lift up the screwdriver to separate the membrane from the meat. If you can get it on one pull, you can get it like an OG. But if it rips, you'll have to repeat the screwdriver slide and lift on the other sections of the rack. When you lift, try not to puncture the flesh. It's not that bad if you stab the meat, though it's worth trying to avoid. But truthfully, when I'm cooking at home, I leave that membrane on.

Seasoning Your Short Ribs

Dry off your short rib rack with a paper or kitchen towel. Spread a thin, even layer of mustard all over the top and sides of the rack, rubbing it in well and making sure there are no clumps. Then season the top and the sides of the rack liberally with the brisket rub. You don't need to season the back where the bone is.

Smoking Your Short Ribs

Follow the instructions in How to Light Your Pit (page 39), aiming for a temperature of 250°F. When the charcoal is ready, start with a hard smoke of oak, using three or four chunks. Let the wood burn off for 5 to 10 minutes.

Now load the short rib rack, fat-side up, into your pit and then watch the temperature. Every time the temperature drops to 240°F, add more oak and charcoal. Once you hit the 3-hour mark on your smoke, start adding a pecan chunk with the oak. Then after the 4-hour mark, you can just go with pecan and charcoal the rest of the way.

If you are wrapping your short ribs. If you want to wrap your short ribs, you can do that once it has a nice bark on it and a deep mahogany color. This will take about 3 hours. If you want to use an instant-read thermometer, you are looking for an internal temperature of around 180°F at the center.

One whole 3-bone beef short rib rack (about 2½ pounds, but sizes vary)

Yellow mustard for rubbing

About ½ cup Bludso's Brisket Rub (page 48)

3 cups water

One 1-ounce packet Lipton dried onion soup mix

Wood: Oak and pecan

Temperature: 240° to 250°F

Rough Cook Time: 4 to 6 hours (But it can really vary, so remember there are no set times.)

Cooking Equipment: Smoker, butcher paper (optional), medium saucepan, BBQ mop or brush

CONTINUED

Beef Short Ribs, continued

If you are not wrapping your short ribs. Once you've got the short rib rack in your pit, in a medium saucepan over medium heat, combine the water and soup mix. Bring to a simmer, stirring once or twice, then remove from the heat. Set this mop aside until you need it.

After about 2½ hours, you can start to mop your short ribs; just make sure you stir the mop each time before you do, as the solids will settle to the bottom. From then on, just mop the ribs every time you open the pit. If your pit flares up a tiny bit, you can use that as an excuse to open it to let out some of the heat and to mop the ribs. Or if your heat is even, you can mop every hour or so.

When you hit the 4-hour mark, you can start checking to see if your short ribs are done. You won't be able to move the bones on a rack the way you can on a rack of pork ribs. But if you give the meat right up against the bone a tug, you should be able to feel if it's ready to pull off. Some folks say you should look for an internal temperature of about 200°F, but that temperature can trick you. You really want to be able to feel that the meat is ready to come off that bone, without it being so tender it'll just fall right off.

Once the short ribs are ready, mop them one last time, then take them out of the pit and set them aside to rest for 30 minutes before carving.

Carving Your Short Ribs

Carving a rack of short ribs is really easy; just cut through the center of the meat between each bone.

Leftover short ribs will keep, well wrapped, in the refrigerator for 5 to 7 days.

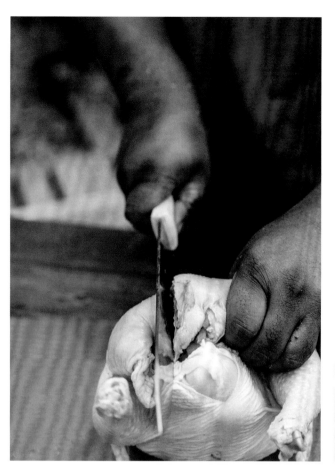

Chicken

BBQ chicken isn't a Texas thing. In fact, back in my day, most BBQ restaurants in Texas didn't have chicken. That's an LA thing, and it's one of the first things you learn to do in your back yard. So here is my twist on the pollo asado–Mexican grilled chicken–sold on the streets of LA. I take those flavors but put some real smoke on them.

Choosing and Prepping a Chicken

Younger chickens are a lot more tender and smoke way better. I don't recommend smoking a chicken that's any bigger than 3½ pounds, and I like to go even smaller if I can.

Place the chicken on your cutting board so the breasts are facing down. Identify the backbone and, using a knife or a pair of poultry shears, cut out and discard the backbone. Flip the bird back over and lay it so it's spread open, with the legs out to the sides. Press down on the breast with your hand—you'll hear the breastbone crack a little—so the chicken is lying mostly flat. Cutting the chicken this way will make for a more even, more consistent smoke.

Seasoning Your Chicken

Dry off the chicken with a paper or kitchen towel. Spread a thin, even layer of mustard all over the chicken, rubbing it in well and making sure there are no clumps. Season the chicken all over with an even sprinkle of black pepper. Follow with an even layer of the chicken rub. Make sure to get the pepper and rub in all the crevices on the sides of the breasts and the legs. Sometimes I tuck the wings back, and sometimes I don't—it's up to you.

CONTINUED

One 3½-pound or smaller whole chicken

Yellow mustard for rubbing

Ground black pepper

About ¼ cup Bludso's Chicken Rub (page 52)

Apple juice for spraying

Wood: Oak, pecan, hickory (optional), and apple

Temperature: 250° to 255°F

Rough Cook Time: 2 to 4 hours (The bigger the chicken, the longer the cook. But remember, there are no set times.)

Cooking Equipment: Smoker, spray bottle, instant-read thermometer (optional)

Note: If you prefer to grill, you could do 3½ pounds extra-large chicken wings instead of the whole chicken; just season as directed for Smoked Chicken Wings (page 111).

Chicken, continued

Smoking Your Chicken

Follow the instructions in How to Light Your Pit (page 39), aiming for a temperature of 255°F. When the charcoal is ready, start with about 70 percent oak and 30 percent pecan. If you want to use hickory, too, you can go with about one-third each oak, pecan, and hickory. Let the wood burn off for 5 to 10 minutes.

Now load the chicken, breast-side up, into your pit. (If you're cooking ribs at the same time, just keep the chicken in a cold spot of your pit.) Watch your temperature. Every time the temperature drops to 250°F, add a little more wood and charcoal, mixing in a little applewood with the rest of it. That one little bit of apple should be enough.

After about 1½ hours of smoking, you can open up the pit and check on the chicken. If the rub is set on the chicken, you can start spraying it with apple juice every time you open the pit. Once you hit the 2-hour mark, you can start checking to see if your chicken is done. If you want, you can check with a thermometer (it should read 150°F in the breast and 165°F in the thigh). But I'm looking for that leg and thigh to be loose—almost to where it bends easily but is still plump. Once you can move it, you know it's ready. If the chicken is not done yet, you only need to cook with pecan and charcoal until it is finished. Spray the chicken with apple juice just before it comes out of the pit, then let it rest for 15 to 20 minutes before carving it.

CONTINUED

Chicken, continued

Carving Your Chicken

You can carve your chicken however you like, but I like to do a classic eight cut. Using your knife, slice the bird down the middle, separating the two sides of the breast. Cut between the legs and the breasts to separate those. You should now have four pieces of chicken. Next chop straight down between the drumstick and the thigh on each leg. Then just cut each breast in half crosswise.

Leftover chicken will keep, well wrapped, in the refrigerator for 5 to 7 days.

Grilled Whole Chicken or Chicken Wings

Set up your grill as instructed in How to Light Your Grill (page 61). Start with about 70 percent oak and 30 percent pecan. If you want to use hickory, too, you can go with about one-third each oak, pecan, and hickory. Let the wood burn off for about 5 minutes, then put the grill grate on the grill.

Place the seasoned whole chicken, skin-side up, or the seasoned chicken wings on the side of the grill away from the charcoal and wood and cover the grill, leaving the vent in the lid above the chicken open. Check the chicken, charcoal, and wood every 30 minutes or so, adding more wood chunks every time they have burned out. On the second load, you can add a chunk of applewood along with the other wood. You should also add more charcoal as needed.

Once the rub is set and the crust looks solid—after 1 hour or so—you can start spraying the chicken with apple juice every time you open the grill to check the chicken and the fire.

If the color on your whole chicken or chicken wings is too dark, open the vent over the charcoal side of the grill (or rotate the lid so the opening is over the charcoal instead of the chicken). If the color keeps getting darker and the chicken hasn't finished cooking, you can go ahead and wrap with butcher paper or aluminum foil and place back on the grill.

For a whole chicken. If you think your chicken is done, you can check it with a thermometer if you want (150°F in the breast and 165°F in the thigh). But I'm looking for that leg and thigh to be loose—almost to where it bends easily but is still plump. Once you can move it, you know it's done. Spray the chicken with apple juice just before it comes off the grill, then let it rest for 15 to 20 minutes before carving as directed.

For chicken wings. The wings are done when you can feel that loose, easy bend in the joint. If they're still really tight, they aren't ready yet. Once they're done—when the joint bends without too much fight or a thermometer stuck into the meatiest part reads 165°F—just spray them with apple juice, take off the grill, and serve them up.

Wood: Oak, pecan, hickory (optional), and apple

Temperature: Medium-low, indirect heat

Rough Cook Time: 1½ to 2 hours for a whole chicken; 1 to 1½ hours for chicken wings

Cooking Equipment: Charcoal grill, spray bottle, butcher paper or aluminum foil (optional), instant-read thermometer (optional)

FLIPPING THE SCRIPT

This chapter has my twist on a few things. To me, anything to which you add the right amount of smoke can turn out special. When you do it right, a Smoked Lamb Leg will make you the legendary pit boss in your family. For me, it's important to always respect the original cultures of the foods that I love, but at the same time I like to also add just a hint of smoke to dishes such as Smoked Oxtails Birria to make them special.

Smoked Lamb Leg

Nobody really cooked this when I was growing up. This recipe is just me and my palate. I like to taste different things, and I love lamb chops. Smoke goes with everything—brisket, pork, a blunt—so why not smoke a lamb leg? Here's my twist on a BBQ lamb leg.

Choosing a Lamb Leg

I look for a lamb leg with a nice fat cap and some marbling. To me, lamb fat isn't the best-tasting fat, but it does take to smoke really well. You want a lamb leg that's solid—like it's been running sprints—not loose.

Seasoning Your Lamb Leg

Dry off the lamb leg with a paper or kitchen towel. Rub it with an even coating of olive oil and then season moderately with pepper. Follow the pepper with the lamb rub, coating the entire leg generously with the seasoning and gently rubbing it in. You want a nice, solid, even layer with no clumps. Add the rosemary leaves, dispersing them evenly and then gently rubbing them in.

Smoking Your Lamb Leg

Follow the instructions in How to Light Your Pit (page 39), aiming for a temperature of 245°F. When the charcoal is ready, start with a light smoke of 70 percent pecan and 30 percent oak. Let the wood burn off for 5 to 10 minutes.

Now load the lamb leg, fat-cap up, into your pit and then watch the temperature. Every time the temperature drops below 240°F, add a little more wood and charcoal.

When you've got the lamb leg in your pit, in a medium saucepan over medium heat, combine the water and soup mix. Bring to a simmer, stirring once or twice, then remove from the heat and set this mop aside until you need it.

After about 2½ hours, if the rub is set, you can start to mop your lamb; just make sure you stir the mop each time before you do, as the solids will settle to the bottom. From then on, mop it every time you open the pit. If your pit flares up a tiny bit, you can use that as an excuse to open it to let out some of the heat and to mop the lamb. Or if your heat is even, you can mop every hour or so.

Once you get to the 3-hour mark, you can add a small amount of applewood to the fire. From then on, it's just pecan and charcoal the rest of the way. The lamb is done when a thermometer inserted into the center (not touching bone) registers 160° to 165°F. When the lamb is ready, mop it one last time, then take it out of the pit and set it aside to rest for 30 minutes before carving.

Carving Your Lamb Leg

I like to hold the leg with the end of the bone pointed straight up, like at a churrascaria, and then cut slices straight down off it.

Leftover lamb will keep, well wrapped, in the refrigerator for 5 to 7 days.

One 5- to 7-pound bone-in lamb leg

Olive oil or yellow mustard for rubbing

Ground black pepper

About 1½ cups Bludso's Lamb Rub (page 51)

Leaves from 2 sprigs rosemary

3 cups water

One 1-ounce packet Lipton dried onion soup mix

Wood: Pecan, oak, and apple

Temperature: 240° to 245°F

Rough Cook Time: About 45 minutes per 1 pound (It can really vary, depending on the lamb leg and your desired internal temperature.)

Cooking Equipment: Smoker, medium saucepan, mop or brush, instant-read thermometer

Smoked Oxtails Birria

I always think about an old Black lady in Waco who used to make Mexican food. She would make good-ass tamales and menudo and all that, and I was just like, "Wow." That was just incredible to me.

I respect the food of other cultures, and Mexican food is one of my favorites, so for me it's important to take it and respect it but also to make it my own thing. I love oxtails, I love menudo, and I love birria. So this is my twist, which puts them all together but also smokes the oxtails. Come on. It's a no-brainer.

This recipe also doubles, triples, and quadruples great for a big party. It's almost just as easy to make a triple batch as it is a single batch.

MAKES 6 TO 8 SERVINGS

BIRRIA

5 pounds oxtails (see Note)

¼ cup Bludso's Steak Rub (page 48)

5½ quarts water

6 tablespoons chicken bouillon powder

1½ cups diced white onions, plus 1 white onion, halved

½ cup minced garlic, plus 20 garlic cloves

2 pounds pigs' feet

1 to 1½ pounds smoked pork jowl

1 to 2 bay leaves

9 guajillo chiles, stemmed and seeded

4 ancho chiles, stemmed and seeded

2 serrano chiles, stemmed (and seeded, if you want less heat)

1 large tomato

Canola oil for brushing

3 tablespoons chopped fresh cilantro

2 tablespoons dried Mexican oregano

¼ teaspoon dried marjoram

¼ teaspoon ground cumin

2 teaspoons distilled white vinegar

1 teaspoon kosher salt

Diced white onion, chopped fresh cilantro, lime wedges, and taco-size corn tortillas and canola oil (if making tacos) for serving

To make the birria: Season the oxtails liberally with the steak rub, making sure to coat them well. Allow to rest at room temperature for at least 1 hour, or in the refrigerator for up to 24 hours.

Follow the instructions in How to Light Your Pit (page 39), aiming for a temperature of 250°F. When the charcoal is ready, add four oak chunks and three pecan chunks and let the wood burn off for 5 to 10 minutes. (Don't use a log unless you plan to BBQ something else, or it will be a waste of a big log.)

Now load the oxtails into your pit and then watch your temperature. Any time it drops below 250°F, add a little more wood and charcoal. Smoke the oxtails for 1 to 2 hours, depending on how deep of a smoke you want. (On a commercial pit, 1 hour is enough, while on a home pit, 2 hours should be plenty. Any longer and the smoke flavor will be too strong.) When the oxtails are ready to pull off, they should be a deep mahogany color. They will not be fully tender yet and will finish cooking in the broth.

While the oxtails are smoking, in a large pot, combine the 5½ quarts water, bouillon powder, diced onions, minced garlic, pigs' feet, pork jowl, and bay leaves. (The pot should be only about half full, leaving enough room for the ingredients that will be added later). Bring to a full boil over high heat, then turn the heat to a gentle simmer, cover the pot, and let simmer until the pig feet are tender but not quite ready to fall apart, about 1 hour.

When the oxtails are finished, take them off the pit and set aside. Now, put the onion halves; guajillo, ancho, and serrano chiles; and tomato on a sheet pan and brush them lightly with canola oil. Place the pan in the pit and smoke for 10 minutes, then pull from the pit and set aside.

Using tongs, remove the pigs' feet and jowl from the pot and discard (or save for another use). You can leave the pigs' feet in the birria if you want, and it will taste great, but that fat is not a good look; so I usually take it out if I'm trying to present it. Taste the broth; it should already taste salty and flavorful. Add the oxtails to the pot, re-cover, and return the liquid to a simmer.

In a medium saucepan over medium heat, combine the smoked guajillo and ancho chiles with water to cover and bring to a simmer. Cook until fully softened, about 10 minutes; then drain, discarding the water.

In a blender, working in batches if necessary, combine the guajillo, ancho, and serrano chiles; tomato; onion halves; whole garlic cloves; chopped cilantro; oregano; marjoram; cumin; vinegar; and a little of the broth and blend, adding more broth if needed to achieve a smooth mixture. Taste the mixture (it should taste pretty good as is) and then add it to the pot. Stir well and then taste the broth. It can be a touch underseasoned, as it will reduce, concentrating the flavor, as it continues to cook.

Re-cover the pot and simmer, stirring occasionally, until the oxtails are tender and the meat comes easily off the bones, about 2 hours. Be careful not to overcook the oxtails, or all of the flavor in the meat will go into the broth. Taste for seasoning, then adjust with the salt if needed.

If serving as a soup. Ladle into bowls, garnish with diced onion and cilantro and pass lime wedges on the side.

If serving as tacos. Make sure to cook your tortillas; don't go through this long cooking process and fuck it up with some dry tortillas. Pull the meat from the oxtails. In a medium skillet over medium-high heat, warm a little canola oil. For each taco, dip a tortilla in the broth, then fry it in the oil for about 10 seconds on each side. Transfer the tortilla to a plate, top with the pulled oxtail meat, diced onion, and cilantro, fold in half, and accompany with a lime wedge.

Leftover birria will keep in an airtight container in the refrigerator for up to 6 days. If you have leftover broth, try it out with your favorite menudo recipe. It will be excellent.

Wood: Oak and pecan

Temperature: 250°F

Rough Cook Time: 1 to 2 hours

Cooking Equipment: Smoker, large pot with a lid, a sheet pan (ideally perforated), blender, medium saucepan, medium skillet (if making tacos)

Note: **Oxtails usually come mixed up in packs at the grocery store, so make sure you are mostly getting pieces that are at least a couple of inches thick.**

Spicy Curried Oxtails

This is my take on the Jamaican and other Caribbean food that I ate when I was growing up—I've got a lot of Belizean in-laws in my family. I use curry paste *and* powder because I like the deep flavor.

The oxtails are browned and simmered in broth before finishing in the curry. You can add potatoes and carrots (I like five medium potatoes and eight large carrots); just put in the skillet with the curry paste and let them cook for the last hour or so.

MAKES 6 TO 8 SERVINGS

About 9 pounds oxtails
(see Note, page 101)

Garlic salt

Ground black pepper

¾ cup chicken bouillon powder

1 tablespoon Kitchen Bouquet,
plus 1 teaspoon

½ cup vegetable oil

1 cup finely chopped yellow onion

4 tablespoons finely chopped garlic

1 habanero chile (optional)

1 cup all-purpose flour

2 tablespoons Jamaican
curry powder

1 tablespoon cayenne pepper

8 cups warm water

One 3.9-ounce package S&B Golden
Curry (I like it hot), or ½ cup Japanese
curry paste of your choice

Cooking Equipment: Large, roasting
pan (big enough to fit the oxtails in
a single layer) with a lid or aluminum
foil; large, deep skillet or Dutch oven
with a lid

Preheat the oven to 350°F.

Liberally season the oxtails all over with garlic salt and black pepper.

While the oven heats, pour water to a depth of about ¾ inch into a large, deep roasting pan. The pan must be large enough to hold the oxtails in a single layer, and there must be enough liquid to almost submerge the oxtails without overflowing. Add ½ cup of the bouillon powder and the 1 tablespoon Kitchen Bouquet and whisk to combine.

Place a large, deep skillet or Dutch oven over medium-high heat and add the vegetable oil. When the oil is shimmering, working in batches if necessary, add the oxtails and cook, turning as needed, until browned on all sides, 5 to 7 minutes for each batch. As each batch is ready, transfer to the roasting pan with the broth, leaving all the fat in the skillet. When all the oxtails are in the roasting pan, remove the skillet from the heat and reserve. Top the oxtails evenly with ½ cup of the onion and 2 tablespoons of the garlic. Cover the pan with a lid or aluminum foil, transfer to the oven, and cook until the oxtails are just fork-tender, about 2½ hours.

Meanwhile, return the skillet with the fat to medium heat. Add the remaining ½ cup onion, 2 tablespoons garlic, 1 teaspoon Kitchen Bouquet, and the habanero (if using) and cook, stirring, for 2 minutes. Add the flour, curry powder, cayenne, and remaining ¼ cup bouillon powder and cook, stirring constantly, until well mixed and the flour is nice and toasted, about 5 minutes. Add the warm water, a little at a time, while stirring constantly to maintain a smooth, unified mixture with no clumps. Once all of the water is incorporated, add the curry paste and whisk to combine. Turn the heat to a bare simmer, cover the pan, and cook, stirring occasionally, until just thickened, about 20 minutes. Then remove from the heat and set aside, covered, until the oxtails have finished cooking in the oven.

Transfer the oxtails to the curry. Turn the heat to a gentle simmer, add 3 cups of the broth from the roasting pan, and stir. Turn the heat to low, cover, and cook until the oxtails are completely tender, about 1 hour. Make sure to stir occasionally, if the curry gets too thick, add a splash of broth.

Spoon the oxtails and their curry into bowls and serve hot.

Leftover curried oxtails will keep in an airtight container in the refrigerator for up to 6 days.

LA Tips

Everything we do at Bludso's, we take the time to do right. We're fucking scientists. We get in the lab and come up with something good. This recipe was an idea we had that's become a hit in our restaurants. We smoke the rib tips good, and you want to eat them as soon as they come off the smoker. But hold up! First, we're gonna fry 'em and put 'em in some good hot sauce, then, BAM, you got some LA tips. They're cool for watching the game and all that. These smoked, fried, and sliced rib tips tossed in our wing sauce are really something special.

Season the rib tips evenly and lightly with the Brisket rub. (They don't need much seasoning or marinating time, as they'll get plenty of seasoning from the Buffalo sauce.)

Follow the instructions in How to Light Your Pit (page 39), aiming for a temperature of 250°F. When the charcoal is ready, add four oak chunks and three pecan chunks. Let the wood burn off for 5 to 10 minutes.

Now load the rib tips, meaty-side up, into your pit and then watch your temperature. Any time it drops below 250°F, add a little more wood and charcoal. Smoke the rib tips until they are a mahogany color and are almost fully cooked, about 2 hours. They should be tender but still have a little tightness to them, as they'll finish cooking in the deep-fryer.

To make the Buffalo sauce: Meanwhile, in a medium saucepan over medium heat, combine the butter, hot sauce, cayenne, and bouillon powder and bring just to a simmer. Remove from the heat and whisk thoroughly to mix well. Pour into a large bowl and set aside.

Once the rib tips are out of the smoker, let them rest for about 15 minutes before frying. (If you are going to fry them up at a later date, you can chill them, whole or sliced, in the fridge and then fry them right before it's time to eat.)

When you're ready to fry the rib tips, in a deep-fryer or deep, heavy pot, pour peanut oil to a depth of about 2 inches, making sure that the rib tips will be fully submerged, and heat to 350°F.

Using a sharp, heavy knife, cut the rib tips into ¼- to ½-inch-thick medallions. You might have to use a little muscle to get through some of the bones and cartilage. Working in batches to avoid crowding, add the medallions to the hot oil and fry until the edges are golden and crispy, 2 to 2½ minutes. Using a slotted utensil or fry basket, scoop them out of the oil and drain well. Add to the Buffalo sauce, toss to coat, and serve immediately. They taste great as is, but if you want a little side something, Bludso's BBQ Sauce and celery are nice additions.

Repeat until all the medallions are fried, always allowing the oil to return to 350°F before adding the next batch.

MAKES 6 TO 8 SERVINGS

6 pounds rib tips (about 4 whole tips)

1 tablespoon Bludso's Brisket Rub (page 48)

BUFFALO SAUCE

1 cup unsalted butter

1 cup hot sauce (I like Frank's RedHot for this)

1 teaspoon cayenne pepper

1 teaspoon chicken bouillon powder

Peanut oil for deep-frying

Bludso's BBQ Sauce (page 54) and celery sticks for serving (optional)

Wood: Oak and pecan

Temperature: 250°F

Rough Cook Time: About 2 hours

Cooking Equipment: Smoker; medium saucepan; deep-fryer or deep, heavy pot and deep-frying thermometer

Smoked Tri-Tip Tacos with Pico de Gallo and Guacamole

Yeah, tri-tip can be done straight on the grill, but I really like cooking it over a high-heat, quick smoke. It is a lean meat, so I cook it quickly to medium-rare and then take it off the pit and let it carry over to medium. I also like to marinate my tri-tip for at least 2 hours but preferably for 24 hours.

And please, please cook your damn corn tortillas in some kind of fat. They need hot grease and a quick cook done right before you eat them. You should be eating tri-tip on a warm tortilla, not one that's been sitting out. Have your pico de gallo and your guacamole ready, so when your tri-tip is done, you can just fry up the tortillas and have your tacos ready to go.

This is the pico de gallo that Noah made for me one time for some brisket tacos, and I knew we had to have it in the book. We both like it very spicy, so use less serrano if you want it to have less heat. Make it just after you make the guacamole and leave it at room temperature until you are ready to make the tacos. It is also used for the breakfast burritos on page 212.

MAKES 4 SERVINGS

Dry off your tri-tip with a paper or kitchen towel. Spread the mustard in a thin, even layer all over the tri-tip, then sprinkle generously with the steak rub and pat gently to set it in place. Put the tri-tip into a large, resealable plastic bag or container. In a small bowl, stir together the orange juice, onion, cilantro, garlic, and oregano. Pour this marinade over the tri-tip, making sure the meat is evenly coated, and seal the bag or tightly cover the container. Refrigerate for at least 2 hours or up to 24 hours.

Follow the instructions in How to Light Your Pit (page 39), aiming for a temperature of 250°F. When the charcoal is ready, add some pecan or whatever wood is prevalent in your area. Let the wood burn off for 5 to 10 minutes.

Remove the tri-tip from its marinade, allowing the marinade to drain off, then discard the marinade. Load the tri-tip into your pit and smoke at 250°F for 1 hour.

After 1 hour, check the internal temperature of your tri-tip with a thermometer; it should be around 100°F. Flip the tri-tip upside down, then use charcoal to raise the temperature of your smoker to 300°F, adding more wood only if the temperature drops to 275° F. Continue cooking until the tri-tip is cooked to your desired temperature. I like mine pulled off when the internal temperature is between 135° and 140°F, 30 to 40 minutes more. Let rest for about 15 minutes; while it rests, the residual heat will increase the temperature to medium (140° to 150°F).

CONTINUED

One 2½- to 3-pound tri-tip

1 tablespoon yellow mustard

About ¼ cup Bludso's Steak Rub (page 48)

1 cup fresh orange juice

½ cup finely chopped white onion

¼ cup finely chopped fresh cilantro

1 tablespoon finely chopped garlic

1 tablespoon dried Mexican oregano

Vegetable or corn oil for frying

12 taco-size corn tortillas

Kosher salt

Pico de Gallo (recipe follows) for serving

Guacamole (recipe follows) for serving

Wood: Pecan or wood of choice

Temperature: 250°F to start; 275° to 300°F

Rough Cook Time: 1½ to 1¾ hours

Cooking Equipment: Smoker, instant-read thermometer, medium skillet

Smoked Tri-Tip Tacos with Pico de Gallo and Guacamole, continued

While the meat is resting, place a medium skillet over medium-high heat and add enough vegetable oil to heavily coat the bottom of the pan. When the oil is shimmering, add the tortillas, one at a time, and fry, turning once, for about 20 seconds on each side. They should be tender and just starting to crisp around the edges. As the tortillas are ready, stack them on one end of a clean kitchen towel and cover with the other end of the towel to keep warm.

Using a sharp knife, slice the tri-tip against the grain about ¼ inch thick. Season the slices with a sprinkle of salt. Lay a long tri-tip slice across the center of each tortilla. Top with a spoonful each of pico de gallo and guacamole, fold in half, and serve immediately.

Leftover tri-tip will keep, well wrapped, in the refrigerator for up to 5 days.

Pico de Gallo

MAKES ABOUT 3 CUPS

1½ pounds ripe tomatoes, cored and finely chopped

3 tablespoons finely chopped serrano chile

¼ cup plus 1 tablespoon finely chopped fresh cilantro

¾ cup finely chopped white onion

1 tablespoon fresh lime juice

Kosher salt

In a medium bowl, combine all the ingredients and stir to mix well, then taste. It should be salty, spicy, and bright. Adjust the seasoning if needed. Transfer to an airtight container and store in the refrigerator for up to 5 days.

Guacamole

MAKES ABOUT 1½ CUPS

2 medium avocados

3 tablespoons finely chopped white onion

2 teaspoons finely chopped serrano chile

1½ teaspoons fresh lime juice

½ teaspoon garlic powder

Kosher salt

Halve and pit the avocados. Using a spoon, scoop the flesh into a medium bowl. Add the onion, chile, lime juice, garlic powder, and a sprinkle of salt and mash gently with a fork until you have your desired texture. Taste for seasoning and adjust with salt if needed. Unless you are eating it right away, cover the bowl tightly with plastic wrap, pressing it down directly onto the surface of the guacamole to prevent browning. The guacamole is best when eaten the same day it is made, but it will keep in the fridge for a couple days if necessary.

Smoked Chicken Wings

Neither my mom nor my granny cooked wings, but wings are *my* thing. They're great for tailgating. Even for smoking, it's a quick smoke, though you've still got to give them the time and babysit them a little.

I don't like big wings on frying, but I do on smoked. You don't want those little Tweety Bird wings.

Seasoning Your Chicken Wings

Dry off your wings with a paper or kitchen towel. Spread a thin, even layer of mustard all over each wing, rubbing it in well and making sure there are no clumps. Season the wings liberally with rub and sprinkle with pepper.

Smoking Your Chicken Wings

Follow the instructions in How to Light Your Pit (page 39), aiming for a temperature of 260°F. When the charcoal is ready, add 70 percent oak and 30 percent pecan. Let the wood burn off for 5 to 10 minutes.

Now load the wings into your pit and then watch your temperature. Every time the temperature drops down to 250°F, add a little more wood and charcoal. On that first drop in temperature, you can add a little applewood if you like.

When the rub has set on the wings—after about 1 hour—you can spray the wings with apple juice every time you open the pit to check on them or the fire.

Continue smoking the wings until they have a little bit of give on the joint and are fully cooked through, about 2½ hours. Spray them with apple juice just before they come out of the pit and then serve.

Leftovers wings will keep in an airtight container in the refrigerator for up to 6 days.

Large chicken wings

Yellow mustard for rubbing

Bludso's Chicken Rub (page 52) for seasoning

Finely or coarsely ground black pepper

Apple juice for spraying

Wood: Oak, pecan, and apple (optional)

Temperature: 250° to 260°F

Rough Cook Time: About 2½ hours

Cooking Equipment: Smoker, spray bottle

Spicy Wood-Grilled Chicken

I love street food if it's done right. When I travel, I want to know the street scene, as that's where some of the best food is. So here is my spin on the pollo asado from the streets of LA, which I have mixed with some flavors of Cuba and the Yucatán, marinated, and then grilled over wood and charcoal. (For my smoker version of pollo asado, see page 89).

MAKES 6 TO 10 SERVINGS

2½ tablespoons achiote paste

2 medium oranges, peeled and quartered

1 cup loosely packed fresh cilantro leaves

1 small or ½ medium red or orange bell pepper, seeded and coarsely chopped

1 small or ½ medium white onion, coarsely chopped

2 serrano chiles, stemmed

3 garlic cloves

1 cup water

½ cup soy sauce

¼ cup cider vinegar

16 chicken pieces (thighs, wings, and drumsticks in any combination)

About ½ cup Bludso's Chicken Rub (page 52)

Ground black pepper

2 tablespoons ground cumin

Wood: Pecan or other mellow wood, such as peach

Temperature: Medium-low, indirect heat

Rough Cook Time: 50 to 70 minutes

Cooking Equipment: Blender, charcoal grill, instant-read thermometer

In a blender, working in batches if needed, combine the achiote paste, oranges, cilantro, bell pepper, onion, chiles, garlic, water, soy sauce, and vinegar and blend until smooth. Set this marinade aside.

Season the chicken pieces liberally with the rub and black pepper, then transfer to a medium bowl and toss with the cumin. Put the chicken into a large, resealable plastic bag or a large container, pour the marinade over the chicken, and coat the chicken evenly. Seal the bag or cover the container and refrigerate for at least 3 hours or for up to 24 hours.

When it's time to cook, set up your grill for medium-low, indirect heat as instructed in How to Light Your Grill (page 61). When the charcoal is ready, add a few pecan chunks and let the wood burn off for about 5 minutes. Lightly coat the grill grate with nonstick cooking spray, then put the grill grate on the grill.

Remove the chicken pieces from the marinade, allowing the marinade to drain off, and place them on the side of the grill away from the charcoal and wood. Discard the marinade. Cover the grill, leaving the vent above the chicken pieces open. Check the charcoal and wood after about 30 minutes, adding more wood and charcoal if needed. You'll need to flip the chicken pieces over about halfway through cooking, so this is a good time to do that as well. Smoke the chicken until fully cooked, 50 to 70 minutes. You can check it with a thermometer, which should read 165°F in the meatiest part. Remove the chicken from the grill, allow to rest briefly, and then serve.

Leftover chicken will keep in an airtight container in the refrigerator for up to 5 days.

Grilled Steak

I like a bone-in, 1½-inch-thick rib-eye. The thicker the steak, the more time there will be for the smoke flavor to get into the meat. That's my favorite steak, but you should use whatever cut you like best. And be smart about how hot you're cooking; the thicker the steak, the lower the heat.

MAKES 1 OR 2 SERVINGS

Room-temperature salted butter
for rubbing, plus 5 tablespoons

Steak cut of your choice

Bludso's Steak Rub (page 48)
for seasoning

2 tablespoons finely chopped garlic

Wood: Pecan

Temperature: Medium-low,
indirect heat

Rough Cook Time: 7 to 10 minutes

Cooking Equipment: Charcoal grill,
small saucepan, basting brush,
instant-read thermometer

Rub room-temperature butter all over your steak, using just enough to get a thin coating. Liberally season your steak all over with rub, coating it well. If it's a bone-in steak, season a little heavier on the end with the bone. I like to season my steak at least 1 hour before cooking, and sometimes up to 1 day in advance.

When you're ready to cook, set up your grill for medium-low, indirect heat as instructed in How to Light Your Grill (page 61). When the charcoal is ready, add two pecan chunks and let the wood burn off for about 5 minutes, then put the grill grate on the grill.

Lay the steak over the direct heat, allowing it to kiss the heat for just about 5 seconds on each side. Then move the steak to the opposite side of the grill (far away from the charcoal and wood), cover the grill, and cook for 5 minutes.

Meanwhile, in a small saucepan over low heat, combine the remaining 5 tablespoons butter and the garlic and warm just until the butter melts, then set aside.

After the steak has been cooking for 5 minutes, begin basting it intermittently with the garlic butter. Keep an eye on your fire and add another pecan chunk and more charcoal as needed. When the steak is about half-cooked (about 40 degrees below your target internal temperature), flip it, baste it, re-cover, and allow it to continue smoking until it reaches your desired internal temperature.

I like my steak medium, so I take it off around 130°F (or closer to 120°F if you are using a thinner steak), then allow it to rest and let the residual heat carry it along. Once the steak reaches the temperature you want, lay it directly over the heat until the underside gets a nice color to it. (This will happen very quickly, so don't worry too much about increasing the internal temp on a thicker, bone-in steak.) Then flip it and get that same color on the second side. Let the steak rest for about 15 minutes before serving.

Leftover steak will keep, tightly covered, in the refrigerator for up to 6 days.

Spicy Hot Dog Chili

There used to be a place in Watts called Jordan's that made my favorite chili dogs in the world. My mom would come home with those sweaty-ass bags. I started to do my own take on them in college, and people still ask about them to this day. Kids love them, and grown-ups do too. I love this chili on an all-beef hot dog with cheddar cheese, chopped onions, and pickled jalapeños. But you can eat it on a hot link or a chili cheeseburger.

This is a wet chili that's mainly for hot dogs. In other words, it's a condiment chili, not a chili you just eat out of a bowl, and it's also way easier to cook.

Most butchers know what chili meat is if you ask for it, but what you really want is a very coarsely ground beef with a lot of fat in the grind.

MAKES ABOUT 2½ QUARTS

2 tablespoons vegetable oil

3 pounds coarsely ground beef

¼ cup finely chopped yellow onion

2 tablespoons finely chopped garlic

2 cups water

2 tablespoons beef bouillon powder

½ cup dark chili powder

2 tablespoons ground cumin

1½ tablespoons cayenne pepper

4 teaspoons seasoning salt

1½ teaspoons ground black pepper

1 teaspoon mustard powder

1 tablespoon cider vinegar

1½ teaspoons ground allspice

1½ teaspoons packed dark brown sugar

¼ cup ketchup

1 tablespoon yellow mustard

1½ cups tomato paste

Cooking Equipment: Large skillet with a lid, medium saucepan

Place a large skillet over medium-high heat and warm the vegetable oil. When the oil is shimmering, add the beef and then the onion and garlic. Cook, stirring and breaking up the meat with a wood spoon, until all of the redness is cooked out of the beef, about 5 minutes.

Meanwhile, in a medium saucepan over medium-low heat, combine the water and bouillon powder, stirring until the powder dissolves. Keep this broth warm over low heat.

When the beef is ready, add the chili powder, cumin, cayenne, seasoning salt, black pepper, and mustard powder and stir to mix well. Taste for seasoning and adjust if needed. Add the vinegar, allspice, brown sugar, and warm beef broth and stir to mix well. Then stir in the ketchup, yellow mustard, and tomato paste, again mixing well. Cover, turn the heat to low, and simmer, stirring occasionally, until the meat is tender and the flavors are totally blended, about 30 minutes, before serving.

Leftover chili will keep in an airtight container in the refrigerator for up to 1 week, or in the freezer for up to 3 months.

Red Chili Burritos

There was a place in Watts called Emil's that had the best red chili burrito in the world—all meat. Mom loved this spot and would pick up burritos for us, and my dad loved it too. After my parents got divorced, my dad would pick us up and get us burritos and soda, and we would eat them at Will Rogers Park on 103rd and Central. My mom learned how to make the burritos, and I just fell in love with the process. I always wanted to achieve the recipe, and respect another culture by doing it right. I love red chili burritos to this day.

This recipe makes enough for 8 extra-large burritos, or about 12 large burritos (depending on how large of tortillas you can find). You can scale this recipe up or down as you like. It freezes so well that I always make a bigger batch.

To make the red chili: In a large, heavy stockpot over medium-high heat, warm the vegetable oil. When the oil is shimmering, add the beef, seasoning salt, 2 tablespoons of the cumin, chili powder, black pepper, granulated onion, and granulated garlic and stir to mix well. Then add 2 cups of the chopped onion and the ½ cup chopped garlic, stir to combine, and cook, stirring occasionally, until the beef is fully browned, 4 to 5 minutes.

Drain off any excess fat from the pot, then add the water, bay leaf, and bouillon powder; stir well; and bring to a boil. Turn the heat to low, cover, and simmer until the meat is nearly tender, about 1 hour. Taste for seasoning and adjust with bouillon powder if needed.

Meanwhile, preheat the oven to 350°F. Lightly oil a baking sheet and arrange the dried chiles in a single layer. Place in the oven until toasted but not blackened, 5 to 10 minutes.

As the chiles are toasting, fill a large saucepan with water, place over medium-low heat, and bring to a gentle simmer. When the chiles are ready, transfer them to the hot water and stir, then leave in the water until softened, about 10 minutes. Drain the chiles, discarding the water.

In a blender, combine the softened chiles, tomato, serranos, remaining ½ cup chopped onion, remaining 2 tablespoons chopped garlic, remaining 1 tablespoon cumin, cilantro, oregano, salt, cayenne, cinnamon, and vinegar. Add about 4 cups broth from the simmering beef mixture and blend until completely smooth. (Depending on the size of your blender, you may need to do this in two batches; add more broth if needed.) There should be no chunks of dried chile or other bits in the mixture. (If you cannot get it perfectly smooth, pass it through a fine-mesh sieve.)

CONTINUED

MAKES 8 SERVINGS

RED CHILI

½ cup vegetable oil

4 pounds beef stew meat (such as chuck), cut into 1-inch pieces

3 tablespoons seasoning salt

3 tablespoons ground cumin

2 tablespoons dark chili powder

1 teaspoon ground black pepper

½ teaspoon granulated onion

½ teaspoon granulated garlic

2½ cups finely chopped white onions

½ cup finely chopped garlic, plus 2 tablespoons

3½ quarts water

1 bay leaf

2 tablespoons chicken bouillon powder, or as needed

8 ounces dried red chiles (such as New Mexico or guajillo), stemmed and seeded

1 medium tomato, cored and coarsely chopped

2 serrano chiles, stemmed and coarsely chopped

¼ cup chopped fresh cilantro

2 tablespoons dried Mexican oregano

1 tablespoon kosher salt

1 teaspoon cayenne pepper

1-inch piece cinnamon stick, coarsely chopped

2 tablespoons distilled white vinegar

Red Chili Burritos, continued

REFRIED BEANS

Two 15-ounce cans refried beans
(ideally chorizo flavored)

½ cup water

1 teaspoon chicken bouillon powder

8 extra-large flour tortillas

4 cups shredded extra-sharp
cheddar cheese

Fresh cilantro for garnishing

Cooking Equipment: Large, heavy
stockpot; baking sheet; large
saucepan; blender; medium
saucepan; large, nonstick skillet

After about 1 hour, add the blended chile mixture in the pot of broth and meat and stir to combine. Re-cover and continue to simmer over low heat until thickened but still moist and the meat is completely tender, about 1 hour longer.

To prepare the refried beans: In a medium saucepan over medium heat, combine the refried beans, water, and bouillon powder, and mix well until warmed through. Keep warm.

In a large, nonstick skillet over medium heat, warm the tortillas, one at a time, just until pliable and easy to roll, about 30 seconds on each side. As the tortillas are ready, stack them on one end of a clean kitchen towel and cover with the other end of the towel to keep warm.

Lay a warm tortilla on a flat surface and add a thin layer of refried beans on the bottom one-third of the tortilla, leaving the edge uncovered. Using a slotted spoon, top with some chili meat and a little of the sauce, then add about ½ cup of the cheddar. Fold in the sides, then fold up the bottom and roll up. Repeat with the remaining tortillas, beans, chili, and cheese. (If you want to make a wet burrito, use the excess sauce to top the rolled burrito, sprinkle with cheese, and warm it in a microwave or conventional oven just to melt the cheese on top.) Garnish with cilantro and serve immediately.

Leftover red chili will keep in an airtight container in the refrigerator for up to 5 days.

Rasheed's Smoked Pork Pho

I met Rasheed Philips when he was a contestant on the first season of *The American Barbecue Showdown,* and we became family. He still reaches out to me, and I reach out to him. It's a trip to be at the point in my career where someone such as Rasheed shows me the respect that he does. He calls me Pops, and I call him Son.

I take it all back to Compton and the young OGs. You've got this young dude, Rasheed, and he's coming in here firm. He's coming in as a soldier, and you just want the best for him. I hate when people are scared to teach someone in their own industry. I always say there's enough for all of us. Rasheed is gonna be a power player in this business, so remember his name.

SMOKED PHO BROTH

5 to 6 pounds smoked pork bones (saved from bone-in smoked butts)

2 medium yellow onions, quartered

4-inch piece fresh ginger, evenly sliced

2-inch piece cinnamon stick

1 tablespoon coriander seeds

1 tablespoon fennel seeds

4 star anise pods

6 garlic cloves

¼ cup fish sauce

Kosher salt

1 Scotch bonnet or habanero chile (optional)

One 6.75-ounce packet rice sticks (also known as rice vermicelli and maifun)

To make the broth: Preheat the oven to 400°F.

Place the pork bones on a baking sheet and roast in the oven until aromatic, 10 to 15 minutes. Remove from the oven and leave the oven on.

Transfer the bones to a large stockpot and set the baking sheet aside. Add enough water to cover the bones comfortably (about 8 quarts) and bring to a boil over high heat, skimming off any impurities that rise to the surface. Turn the heat to a simmer.

Meanwhile, place the onions and ginger on the now-empty baking sheet and place on the top rack of the oven. Roast the onions and ginger, flipping them after 5 to 6 minutes, until evenly browned, 10 to 15 minutes total. Remove from the oven and set aside to cool.

In a small skillet over low heat, combine the cinnamon, coriander seeds, fennel seeds, and star anise and toast, moving the pan constantly, until fragrant, 8 to 10 minutes. Remove from the heat. Turn out the spices onto a square of cheesecloth and tie the corners together with kitchen string to form a bundle. (If you don't have cheesecloth on hand, simply drop them directly into the pot.)

Add the spices to the broth along with the roasted onions and ginger, garlic, fish sauce, and 1½ tablespoons salt. Simmer the broth, uncovered, for 2 hours, continuing to skim off any impurities from the surface. Add the Scotch bonnet and simmer, skimming as needed, for 1 to 3 hours more (the longer you simmer, the more flavor your broth will have).

Remove the pot from the heat, scoop out and discard the bones, and then strain the broth through a fine-mesh sieve and discard the remaining solids. Taste and adjust the seasoning with salt if needed. When it's time to serve, make sure the broth is very hot. Prepare the noodles according to the package directions (usually they are bloomed in hot water).

For each bowl: Evenly divide the noodles among individual bowls. Place the sliced meat on top of the noodles and then ladle the hot broth over the meat and noodles. The broth will warm the meat. Garnish with the cilantro and green onions. Offer the toppings and condiments at the table for diners to add as they like. Eat immediately.

Leftover broth will keep in an airtight container in the refrigerator for up 1 week, or in the freezer for up to 5 months.

FOR EACH BOWL

8 ounces Grilled Steak (page 113) or Beef Short Ribs (page 85), thinly sliced

¼ cup chopped fresh cilantro

¼ cup thinly sliced green onions, white and green parts

TOPPINGS AND CONDIMENTS

Bean sprouts

Fresh mint leaves

Thin jalapeño chile slices

Hoisin sauce

Fish sauce

Lime wedges

Cooking Equipment: Baking sheet, large stockpot, small skillet, cheesecloth and kitchen string (optional)

SOUL
FOOD
SUNDAYS

On Sunday mornings when I was growing up, right after breakfast, the smell of the house went from delightful to amazing. Something baking, something boiling, something smoking, something smothering—there was always *something* special happening on those days. I want to pay homage to my heritage and my family and close friends on Sundays, and this food takes me back.

Red Beans and Rice

This is one of my fall favorites. Having family from Texas—and Louisiana being so close—I always loved seeing how Texans cooked up food from Louisiana and how people from Louisiana cooked up food from Texas. My mom or my granny would always make this dish on a cold day in the fall for the Cowboys games. It just brings back good memories—especially of when I was old enough to be having cognac with Granny and sitting in the recliner.

To be honest, I always think the beans should be able to stand alone in a dish. I don't even like rice with mine. I just like a delicious broth. You should be able to taste the broth when you're cooking, before you've even added in the beans, and know how good it's going to be.

MAKES 4 TO 6 SERVINGS

5 quarts water, or as needed

2 smoked ham hocks

¼ cup chicken bouillon powder, or as needed

2 bay leaves

4 serrano chiles

1 habanero chile (optional)

2 tablespoons vegetable oil

1½ cups finely chopped white onions

1 cup finely chopped celery

1 cup finely chopped green bell pepper

1 pound andouille sausage, sliced into ¼-inch-thick coins

2 pounds dried small red beans or red kidney beans, rinsed and sorted

¼ cup finely chopped garlic

2 tablespoons dark chili powder

1 teaspoon cayenne pepper (optional)

½ teaspoon ground thyme

Cooked extra-long-grain white rice for serving

Chopped parsley for garnishing

Cooking Equipment: Large stockpot, large skillet

In a large stockpot over high heat, combine the water, ham hocks, bouillon powder, bay leaves, serranos, and habanero (if using) and bring to a boil. Turn the heat to low, cover, and let simmer for 1 hour.

Meanwhile, in a large skillet over medium-high heat, warm the vegetable oil. When the oil is shimmering, add the onions, celery, and bell pepper and cook, stirring often, until all the vegetables are wilted, about 6 minutes. Set aside off the heat.

When the ham hocks have been simmering for 30 minutes, taste the broth and adjust the seasoning with additional bouillon powder, if needed. Add the sausage, dried beans, garlic, chili powder, cayenne (if using), and thyme and stir well, Return to a simmer, re-cover, and cook, stirring occasionally, for another 30 minutes. Then add the vegetable mixture, cover, and continue cooking, stirring occasionally, until the ham hocks are soft and falling apart and the beans are fully tender, about 1½ hours. Keep an eye on the water level throughout the cook and add warm water if needed to maintain the level, being careful not to add too much and dilute the broth; which should be nice and thick, like a gravy.

Serve the beans with a big scoop of rice and garnish with a sprinkle of parsley.

Leftovers will keep in an airtight container in the refrigerator for up to 1 week.

Pinto Beans with Smoked Neck Bones

These beans take me back to cold days after school with my mom. She'd go to work at 2:00 a.m. and get back home while I was at school. Then when I got home, she'd be taking a nap, but I'd see everything laid out on the stove, and I knew what we were having for dinner. Then she'd wake up and start cooking pinto beans, and it would fog up all the windows and get me so excited.

I almost like this meal to be like a gravy, where you can barely see the beans–less thick than refried beans but all gelled together with the onion, spoon-tender neck bones, and garlic. To me, great beans like these don't even need rice or cornbread. They're good enough to stand alone. Just remember that cooking the broth is the most critical step. What that tastes like is what the beans will taste like. Also, you don't need to add any salt because the chicken bouillon powder is your salt for the whole pot. But some smoked neck bones are saltier than others, so be careful to taste your broth carefully before adding too much seasoning.

This is an easy recipe, but it's at its best when you take your time with it. It can take 4 or 5 hours to make a pot of these beans, so start them early in the day if you have time.

MAKES 4 TO 6 SERVINGS

In a large stockpot over high heat, combine the water, neck bones, onion, garlic, bouillon powder, and bay leaves and bring to a boil. Cover, turn the heat to a gentle boil, and cook for about 1 hour, allowing the neck bones to begin to cook and flavor the broth.

After the hour, taste the broth for seasoning and add additional bouillon powder, if needed. The broth should already taste delicious. Now add the beans, serranos, chili powder, black pepper, and cayenne and stir to incorporate; turn the heat to low, cover, and simmer until the beans are tender and the broth has thickened up nicely, 2 to 3 hours. Then remove from the heat and allow everything to settle for about 1 hour. The beans will thicken up a little bit more as well.

When ready to serve, ladle the beans with some of the broth into individual bowls, trying to get a little bit of the meat in each bowl as well.

Leftovers will keep in an airtight container in the refrigerator for up to 6 days.

5 quarts water

2 packs smoked pork neck bones (4 to 5 pounds total)

1 medium-to-large yellow onion, finely chopped

3 garlic cloves, chopped

¼ cup chicken bouillon powder, or as needed

2 bay leaves

2 pounds dried pinto beans, rinsed and sorted

3 serrano chiles, stemmed

Heaping 2 tablespoons dark chili powder

¼ teaspoon ground black pepper

1 pinch cayenne pepper

Cooking equipment: Large stockpot

Smothered Turkey Wings

I love Thanksgiving dinner, and my mom knew that. But these smothered turkey wings are the next best thing, and she'd cook 'em up with some rice or cornbread dressing. It's weird cooking a whole turkey when it's not Thanksgiving, but that doesn't mean you can't eat turkey at other times of the year. So this is a way to do it and make a memorable dinner.

It's an amazing dish that takes some time, but it's not that hard to cook. This is a major Sunday meal for me. It's cool when you get old enough to hang out all day and cook turkey wings on a Wednesday. But if you're a young mom or a young couple, you're only gonna take the time to make this for a Sunday dinner. It was hard to get everybody to sit down around the table on most days of the week. But on Sundays, we were always going to sit our asses down and get some dinner, and turkey wings are Sunday dinner.

MAKES 8 SERVINGS

Seasoning salt

Ground black pepper

¼ cup granulated onion

¼ cup granulated garlic

1 tablespoon ground dried sage

1½ teaspoons ground dried thyme

8 large turkey wings, split into flats and drumettes (16 pieces total)

½ cup vegetable oil

4 tablespoons salted butter

1 cup finely chopped yellow onion

½ cup finely chopped celery

1 tablespoon finely chopped garlic

8 cups warm water

2 tablespoons chicken bouillon powder

1½ cups all-purpose flour

One 10½-ounce can condensed cream of chicken soup or cream of mushroom soup

About 8 cups cooked extra-long-grain white rice or cornbread dressing (see page 237)

Cooking Equipment: Large skillet with a lid, large roasting pan (one you would use to roast a turkey) with a lid or aluminum foil

Preheat the oven to 350°F.

In a medium bowl, combine 1 cup seasoning salt, ½ cup pepper, the granulated onion, granulated garlic, sage, and thyme and stir to mix well.

Dry off the turkey wing pieces with a paper or kitchen towel. Season liberally on all sides with the seasoning mix.

Place a large skillet over medium-high heat and add the vegetable oil and butter. When the butter has melted and the fat is hot, working in batches, add the wing pieces in a single layer, being careful not to crowd the pan. They should sizzle the moment they hit the pan. Let them cook, keeping an eye on the heat and adjusting it if needed to make sure they don't burn, until they are golden brown on the underside, about 4 minutes. Once browned, flip them and cook the second side until golden brown, about 3 minutes more. As the wing pieces are browned, transfer to a large roasting pan, arranging them in a single layer and leaving the fat in the pan. Brown the remaining wing pieces the same way. If they don't all fit in a single layer in the roasting pan, you can stack them a bit; just make sure the biggest pieces are on the bottom.

Turn the heat to medium-low. Add the chopped onion, celery, and chopped garlic to the fat remaining in the pan and cook, stirring occasionally, just until translucent, about 3 minutes. Using a slotted spoon, lift the vegetables out of the pan and sprinkle them over the turkey wings. Set the skillet aside.

Pour 2 cups of the water evenly over the turkey wings. Cover the pan with a lid or aluminum foil, then transfer to the oven and cook until the wings are nearly tender, about 2½ hours.

While the wings are cooking, return the skillet to medium-low heat, add the bouillon powder to the fat remaining in the pan, and whisk to combine. Add the flour and whisk constantly just until toasted, 1 to 2 minutes. Add the remaining 6 cups water, a little at a time, while whisking constantly to prevent lumps and build your gravy.

Add the cream of chicken soup to the skillet, turn the heat to low, and then whisk constantly until the mixture has thickened to a medium gravy consistency, about 8 minutes. Taste this gravy and adjust with seasoning salt and pepper if needed. Set aside until the wings are ready.

When the wings are tender, remove the pan from the oven and, using a slotted utensil, transfer the wings to a large plate. Add just enough of the gravy to the broth in the pan to be able to partially submerge the wings and stir to mix. Then return the wings to the pan, flipping them so the side that was up on the first cook is now facing down in the gravy. Re-cover the roasting pan, return it to the oven, and cook the wings until completely tender, 45 minutes to 1½ hours, depending on their size.

Spoon the turkey wings and gravy over the rice and serve immediately, with any remaining gravy on the side.

Leftover smothered turkey wings will keep in an airtight container in the refrigerator for up to 5 days.

Smothered Chicken and Gravy

This is one of my favorite dishes. A lot people think it's hard to make, but it's really not. You actually cook your chicken in the gravy. I love it smothered and just served over mashed potatoes or rice with collard greens on the side.

I don't believe in frying chicken and then serving some house gravy over it. To me, the only way to make this dish is to brown the chicken in the pan and then cook it in the gravy. It's another one of the dishes I use to judge a soul food or Southern restaurant. If I go with friends and one person gets the short rib, one person gets the fried chicken, and I get the smothered chicken, and I see that my chicken is the same as the fried chicken and my gravy is the same as the short rib gravy, I know the kitchen is just using fried chicken and house gravy.

MAKES 4 SERVINGS

4 chicken drumsticks

4 chicken thighs

4 chicken wings

Seasoning salt

Ground black pepper

1 tablespoon garlic powder

1 tablespoon onion powder

½ cup vegetable oil, or as needed

½ cup finely chopped yellow onion

1 teaspoon finely chopped garlic

2 tablespoons finely chopped celery

Two 1-ounce packets Lipton dried onion soup mix

1½ teaspoons Kitchen Bouquet

1 tablespoon chicken bouillon powder, or as needed

½ teaspoon cayenne pepper

1¼ cups all-purpose flour

6 cups warm water

Mashed potatoes (see page 185) or cooked extra-long-grain white rice for serving

Cooking Equipment: Large skillet (big enough to hold all the chicken pieces in a single layer) with a lid

Season all the chicken pieces aggressively on all sides with an even coating of seasoning salt and black pepper. It should be a fairly heavy coating of both. Then season the pieces with the garlic powder and onion powder.

Place a large skillet over medium-high heat and warm the vegetable oil. When the oil is shimmering, add all the chicken pieces in a single layer; they should sizzle the moment they hit the pan. Let the chicken cook, keeping an eye on the heat and adjusting it if needed to make sure they don't burn, until fully browned on the underside, about 10 minutes. Once browned, flip them over, adding more oil as needed, and cook the second side until golden brown, another 6 minutes or so. The chicken will finish cooking in the gravy, so there's no need to worry about it being cooked through at this point. Transfer the chicken pieces to a large plate and set aside.

Turn the heat to medium-low; add the chopped onion, garlic, and celery; and cook, stirring, just until softened, about 2 minutes. Add the soup mix, Kitchen Bouquet, bouillon powder, and cayenne and stir to mix well. Then add the flour and cook, whisking constantly, until this roux is well mixed and nice and toasted, about 3 minutes. (If the roux is getting clumped inside of your whisk, add a little more oil to help it whisk more smoothly.) Add the water, about ½ cup at a time and whisking constantly, until you have a loose, fairly pourable gravy, about 5 minutes. Taste for seasoning and adjust with more bouillon powder if needed.

Return the chicken pieces in a single layer to the pan, submerging them in the gravy. Bring to a simmer, then cover, turn the heat to a low simmer, and cook until the chicken is completely tender, 45 minutes to 1 hour.

Serve immediately, with a scoop of mashed potatoes on the side.

Leftover smothered chicken will keep in an airtight container in the refrigerator for up to 5 days.

Fried Chicken

There are so many ways to make fried chicken, and I've tried nearly all of them. When you get home from work tired, I still want you to be able to cook some bomb fried chicken that'll make your kids go crazy. This recipe will do just that.

If you're new to frying chicken, just fry one thigh to start, let it cool, and then taste it to see if it's undercooked, overcooked, or perfect. Then adjust the timing based on how that piece came out, and you'll have fried chicken mastered in no time.

This recipe yields about twice as much flour as you'll need for the chicken, but I always like to make this much and then save the rest. The extra flour will keep for several months and means you can make excellent fried chicken in less than a half hour.

MAKES 2 TO 4 SERVINGS

Cut the chicken into ten pieces—wings, thighs, drumsticks, and each breast half cut in half crosswise.

In a deep-fryer or deep, heavy skillet, pour vegetable oil to a depth of about 2 inches, making sure that the chicken will be fully submerged, and heat to 350°F. Set a wire rack on a large baking sheet or line a large plate with paper towels and place near the stove.

In a large bowl, combine the flour, black pepper, seasoning salt, granulated onion, granulated garlic, paprika, cayenne, and sage and stir to mix thoroughly. Scoop out and reserve about half of the flour mixture to use another time. You're going to dredge and fry the chicken pieces in batches, so make sure to prepare only as many pieces of chicken at a time as will fit comfortably in your fryer or skillet. I like to fry the white meat with the white meat and the dark meat with the dark meat.

Rinse the chicken under cold running water just to moisten. One at a time, dredge the chicken pieces in the flour mixture, making sure to coat them completely it, then shake off any excess flour.

Gently add the chicken pieces to the hot oil and fry until they form a deep golden brown, crispy crust, 12 to 15 minutes (wings will cook the fastest, and thighs will cook the slowest). Using tongs, transfer the pieces to the prepared baking sheet to drain. Fry the remaining chicken pieces, always allowing the oil to return to 350°F before adding the next batch.

Eat the chicken doused with hot sauce, or with some pickled jalapeños.

The chicken tastes best when eaten right away, but will keep in an airtight container in the refrigerator for up to 5 days.

One 2½- to 3-pound whole chicken

Vegetable oil or melted lard for deep-frying

3 cups all-purpose flour

½ cup ground black pepper

½ cup seasoning salt

2 tablespoons granulated onion

2 tablespoons granulated garlic

1 tablespoon sweet paprika

1½ teaspoons cayenne pepper

½ teaspoon ground dried sage

Hot sauce or pickled jalapeños for serving

Cooking Equipment: Deep-fryer or deep, heavy skillet and deep-frying thermometer

Fried Pork Chop Sandwich

"Fried pork chop sandwich, watch the bone." This was always my go-to as a youngster. I don't think you could even get boneless pork chops back when I was growing up. I used to eat this with regular hot sauce in the mayonnaise, but now I prefer the mayo with Sriracha.

This is something quick. Set up the sandwich shit, drop the pork chop in the fryer, put on the game, and go. That's it. If you want to do it with boneless pork chops you can, but that's not the way we ever did it. "Fried pork chop sandwich, watch the bone." That's it.

MAKES 4 SERVINGS

In a deep-fryer or deep, heavy skillet, pour vegetable oil to a depth of about 2 inches, making sure that the pork chops will be fully submerged, and heat to 350°F. Set a wire rack on a large baking sheet or line a large plate with paper towels and place near the stove.

To make the mayo: While the oil is heating, in a small bowl, combine the mayonnaise and Sriracha and stir until well mixed.

Generously spread the mayo on one side of each bread slice or on the cut sides of the hamburger buns. Have the onion, tomato, and pickle slices and lettuce leaves close by. Put the seasoned flour in a large bowl.

Working with no more than two pork chops at a time, depending on the size of your deep-fryer, rinse the pork under cold running water just to moisten and then season *very* lightly with seasoning salt—like a shadow. One at a time, dredge the chops in the flour, making sure to coat them completely, then shake off any excess flour.

Gently add a pork chop to the hot oil and fry until the golden brown, about 6 minutes. Using tongs, transfer the chop to the prepared baking sheet to drain. If the pork chop is on the thick side, it may still be a little pink on the inside; if you let it sit for a minute or two, the residual heat will cook it a bit more. Put the pork chop on a bread slice or bun and top with onion, tomato, pickle, and/or lettuce. Close the sandwich with a second bread slice or bun top, mayo-side down.

Fry the remaining pork chops, always allowing the oil to return to 350°F before adding the next chop. Make the remaining sandwiches and enjoy.

Fried pork chops are best when eaten right away, but will keep in an airtight container in the refrigerator for up to 5 days.

CONTINUED

Ingredients

Vegetable oil for deep-frying

SPICY MAYO

1 cup mayonnaise

2 tablespoons Sriracha

8 slices white bread, or 4 soft hamburger buns, split

Thinly sliced white onion, tomato slices, sweet or spicy sliced pickles, and/or iceberg lettuce leaves for topping

4 bone-in center-cut pork chops, each about ½- inch thick, untrimmed

About 1 cup Seasoned Flour (page 140)

Seasoning salt

Cooking Equipment: Deep-fryer or deep, heavy skillet and deep-frying thermometer

1 cup all-purpose flour

¼ cup seasoning salt

¼ cup plus 1½ teaspoons
ground black pepper

2 tablespoons granulated onion

2 tablespoons granulated garlic

1½ teaspoons sweet paprika

¼ teaspoon cayenne pepper

Seasoned Flour

In a medium bowl, combine all the ingredients and mix thoroughly. Transfer to an airtight container and store at room temperature for up to 5 months.

Fried Ribs

My cousin Shirley Ann makes the best fried ribs. We would fry them in leftover grease from a fish fry until they were golden brown and then have them in a sandwich.

A lot of people marinate ribs to get them tender, but I don't think you need to. There's always going to be a little bit of a tug when you fry them. Just remember you're going to cut these ribs before frying. Don't try to fry up that whole slab, goddamnit.

MAKES 3 OR 4 SNACK-SIZE, OR 1 OR 2 MAIN-COURSE, SERVINGS

Vegetable oil for deep-frying

One 3½-pound rack St. Louis–cut pork spareribs

About 1 cup Seasoned Flour (facing page)

Cooking Equipment: Deep-fryer or deep, heavy skillet and deep-frying thermometer

In a deep-fryer or deep, heavy skillet, pour vegetable oil to a depth of about 2 inches, making sure that the spareribs will be fully submerged, and heat to 325°F.

While the oil is heating, dry your rib rack with a paper or kitchen towel. Next, flip the rib slab and find the lean flap meat hanging off the center of the back. Using a chef's knife, cut that off. (You can save that meat for Spicy Maple Breakfast Sausage, page 207, if you want.) Then, with the bone side facing up (so you can more easily see the groove on the ribs and find the cut), use the knife to slice down between those ribs in nice, clean cuts, just as you would if they were cooked.

Set a wire rack on a large baking sheet or line a large plate with paper towels and place near the stove. Put the seasoned flour into a large bowl. You're going to fry in batches, so make sure you're only preparing as many ribs at a time as will fit comfortably in your fryer or skillet.

Rinse a rib under cold running water just to moisten lightly. Dredge the rib in the flour, making sure to coat it completely, then shake off any excess flour and gently add it to the hot oil. Repeat with a few more ribs, being careful not to crowd the pan. Fry the ribs until they form a deep golden brown, crispy crust, about 14 minutes. The time can vary depending on your fryer and the thickness of the ribs. Just make sure to pull the ribs out before they get too dark. Using tongs, transfer the ribs to the prepared baking sheet to drain. Continue frying the ribs, always allowing the oil to return to 325°F before adding the next batch.

The ribs are best when eaten right away, but will keep in an airtight container in the refrigerator for up to 5 days.

Sunday Short Ribs

This is one of the staples of soul food. My mom and my grandma could both get down. I never said who made the best (and I never will). This is also one of the dishes that I really judge a soul food restaurant on.

Short ribs, like oxtails, can seem hard to cook, but I'll show you that they're easy. Follow these directions, just listen, and you'll be cooking short ribs for people in no time. Only one thing makes your short ribs tough—not cooking them long enough.

Preheat the oven to 350°F.

Liberally season the tops and sides of the short ribs with seasoning salt, pepper, and granulated onion. You don't need to season the back where the bone is.

Place a large skillet over medium-high heat and warm the vegetable oil. When the oil is shimmering, working in batches, add the short ribs, meat-side down, and cook until browned, about 6 minutes. Then turn the ribs bone-side down and brown for 2 minutes more. Transfer the short ribs, meat-side up, to the roasting pan in a single layer, leaving the fat in the skillet. When all the ribs are in the roasting pan, remove the skillet from the heat and reserve. Top the ribs evenly with the garlic cloves and ¼ cup of the onion.

In a medium saucepan over high heat, combine the cold water and one packet of the soup mix. Whisk thoroughly to combine and bring to a simmer. Remove from the heat and pour over the short ribs, using just enough of the liquid to partially submerge the short ribs. Cover the pan with a lid or aluminum foil, transfer it to the oven, and cook the ribs until just tender, about 3 hours.

Meanwhile, return the skillet with the fat to medium-low heat. Add the chopped garlic and remaining ½ cup onion and stir to combine. Add the bouillon powder, remaining packet of soup mix, and Kitchen Bouquet and stir well. Add the flour and whisk constantly until the flour is nice and toasted, about 3 minutes. Add 4 cups of the warm water, a little at a time, while whisking constantly. Then whisk in more warm water as needed (usually about 2 cups more) for a medium gravy consistency. Bring to a bare simmer and continue simmering, stirring occasionally, for about 10 minutes. Remove this gravy from the heat and set aside while the short ribs continue to cook.

When the short ribs are ready, transfer them to a platter or bowl, leaving the broth in the pan. Add the gravy to the broth, a cup or so at a time, whisking to mix well; use only as much of the gravy as needed to achieve a medium-thick consistency. Return the short ribs, meat-side down, to the roasting pan. Re-cover with the lid or foil, return to the oven, and cook until the ribs are completely tender, about 1 hour.

Serve the short ribs immediately, accompanied by rice or mashed potatoes.

Leftover short ribs will keep in an airtight container in the refrigerator for 4 to 6 days.

MAKES 6 TO 8 SERVINGS

16 pieces meaty, bone-in beef short ribs (6 to 7 pounds)

Seasoning salt

Ground black pepper

Granulated onion for seasoning

¼ cup vegetable oil

8 garlic cloves, plus 2 tablespoons finely chopped

¾ cup finely chopped yellow onion

2½ cups cold water, plus 4 to 6 cups warm water

Two 1-ounce packets Lipton dried onion soup mix

1 tablespoon chicken bouillon powder

1½ teaspoons Kitchen Bouquet

1 cup all-purpose flour

Cooked extra-long-grain white rice or mashed potatoes (see page 185) for serving

Cooking Equipment: Large skillet, 15-inch roasting pan (big enough to fit the ribs in a single layer) with a lid or aluminum foil, small or medium saucepan

Monique's 7-Day Rooster

I gotta give my ex-wife Monique an A for effort because she used to be intimidated by cooking. The truth is, we learned a lot from each other, and now she's a damn good cook. I actually think her gumbo might even be better than mine, which is a shame, because you never want to teach somebody how to come back and kick your ass on your something.

But there was this one day that she was cooking this beautiful dinner for me with all these sides and everything, and I could hear she was frustrated. She said, "I can't get this damn chicken tender!" So I said, "Let me see the package." And she said, "It wasn't in no package. It came in a clear bag!" And I said, "Oh no, Monique, you didn't buy a damn chicken. That's an old-ass stewing rooster!" I laughed my ass off because cooking that shit is like trying to roast your little brother. We still clown about it to this day because those damn things *never* get tender.

MAKES 4 SERVINGS

1 old-ass 6-year-old stewing rooster (if you can't find a 6-year-old rooster, use a tire off a 1978 Oldsmobile)

2 pairs of your granddaddy's socks that he was wearing while walking around in the rain

½ cup chicken bouillon powder

Cooking Equipment: Large stockpot

Put all the ingredients in a large stockpot with some water and let that simmer for 7 days and 7 nights! Serve at your own risk.

CHILLING AT THE LAKE OR THE BEACH

I've cooked a lot of BBQ in my life, but I love seafood. Growing up, I got to eat at some great restaurants in LA but then also got to go up to Fisherman's Wharf in San Francisco with my mom a couple of times. I was nine years old when I went to Mexico with my dad and had my first fish taco, and it was so damn good. I still remember that. Being in California, most of our getaways with our parents were at the ocean or a lake. One of my favorites was going to our fishing spot at the Salton Sea. That's prime chilling—being by the water and cooking outside. Fresh fish that you just caught and cooked is the best-tasting fish there is. So this chapter just pays respect to some of my favorite food in the world.

Oysters BBQ Fella

I love oysters on the half shell, and grew up eating them down in Baja. But then getting to come down to Texas and try some Gulf oysters was damn cool too.

Oysters Rockefeller are one of my favorite foods. Usually I would say if it ain't broke, don't fix it, but then one day I had some oysters and started messing around with them on the pit. So I came up with this little slant on it, and the oysters came out pretty damn good.

MAKES 3 TO 6 APPETIZER SERVINGS

8 slices bacon

¾ cup salted butter

2 tablespoons finely chopped yellow onion

2 teaspoons finely chopped garlic

2 cups loosely packed spinach leaves, chopped

½ cup shredded sharp white cheddar cheese

2 tablespoons whole milk

1 teaspoon fresh lemon juice

12 medium-to-large live oysters in the shell

Old Bay seasoning for sprinkling

Wood: Pecan or other light wood, such as peach

Temperature: 240° to 250°F

Rough Cook Time: 5 to 7 minutes

Cooking Equipment: Smoker, large skillet, medium skillet

Follow the instructions in How to Light Your Pit (page 39), aiming for a temperature of 250°F. When the charcoal is ready, add a few chunks of pecan and let the wood burn off for 5 to 10 minutes.

Meanwhile, line a large plate with paper towels .

In a large skillet over medium-high heat, cook the bacon in a single layer, flipping the slices about halfway through, until crispy and mahogany colored, 8 to 10 minutes. Once the bacon is crispy, transfer it to the prepared plate to drain and cool. Remove the skillet from the heat and reserve the bacon fat.

In a medium skillet over medium heat, melt the butter. Add the onion and garlic and cook, stirring often, just until translucent, about 2 minutes. Add the spinach and cook, stirring occasionally, until wilted, about 5 minutes. Crumble the cooled bacon, add it to the pan, and stir to combine. Then add the cheese, milk, and lemon juice and stir until the cheese is just melted. Remove from heat and set aside.

Shuck the oysters, leaving them on the half shell with as much juice as possible remaining in the shell. Top each oyster with ¼ teaspoon of the reserved bacon fat and a light sprinkle of Old Bay.

Place the oysters in the pit and smoke just until warmed through, 5 to 7 minutes. (You could use a grilling rack or baking sheet to make it easier, but truthfully I just place them individually, directly on the racks.)

Take the oysters from the pit and top each with a generous dollop of the spinach-bacon mixture. Serve immediately.

Grilled Oysters BBQ Fella

Wood: Pecan or other light wood, such as peach

Temperature: Medium-low, indirect heat

Rough Cook Time: 5 to 7 minutes

Cooking Equipment: Charcoal grill

Set up your grill for medium-low, indirect heat as instructed in How to Light Your Grill (page 61). When the charcoal is ready, add a few chunks of pecan. Let the wood burn off for about 5 minutes, then put the grill grate on the grill.

Place the oysters on the side of the grill away from the charcoal and wood and cover the grill, leaving the vent in the lid above the oysters open. Smoke just until warmed through, 5 to 7 minutes. Remove from the grill and top as directed.

Grilled Mojo Shrimp

During my travels shooting *Bar Rescue* with Jon Taffer, I was turned on to so many foods and different cultures, including some incredible Cuban food that I had down in Tampa Bay. Then, of course, going down to the pier in Redondo Beach, or the wharf in San Francisco with my mom, I always loved eating seafood. Here, I put a little spicy mojo twist on our shrimp with smoke on the grill and finish it with a butter dipping sauce—putting all those experiences together into something I love.

To make the mojo sauce: In a blender, combine all of the ingredients and blend until smooth. Set aside 1 tablespoon of the sauce for the Mojo Butter.

When you're about an hour out from wanting to cook, in a large bowl, combine the shrimp and remaining Mojo Sauce and mix until the shrimp are completely coated. Cover and marinate at room temperature for 45 minutes to 1 hour.

When you're ready to cook, set up your grill for a medium-low, direct heat as instructed in How to Light Your Grill (page 61). When the charcoal is ready, add a few chunks of pecan. Let the wood burn off for about 5 minutes, then put the grill grate on the grill.

Remove the shrimp from their marinade, allowing the marinade to drain off, then discard the marinade. Lay the shrimp close to the flame but not quite over it and sprinkle with salt. Cover the grill and grill the shrimp until they are just cooked, 5 to 7 minutes.

To make the mojo butter: While the shrimp are cooking, in a small saucepan over medium-low heat or in a small bowl in the microwave, melt the butter. Remove from the stove top or microwave; add the reserved Mojo Sauce, garlic, soy sauce, and cayenne; and stir to mix.

Serve the shrimp right away, with the Mojo Butter for dipping.

Leftover shrimp will keep in an airtight container in the refrigerator for up to 3 days.

MAKES 4 SERVINGS

MOJO SAUCE

1 cup fresh orange juice

¼ cup fresh lime juice

¼ cup tightly packed fresh cilantro leaves

2 tablespoons finely chopped white onion

1 serrano chile, stemmed and coarsely chopped

½ jalapeño chile, stemmed and coarsely chopped

1½ teaspoons finely chopped garlic

1½ teaspoons dried Mexican oregano

1 teaspoon ground cumin

½ teaspoon kosher salt

1 tablespoon vegetable oil

4 pounds large, shrimp, deveined

Kosher salt

MOJO BUTTER

½ cup salted butter

1 tablespoon Mojo Sauce (above)

½ teaspoon finely chopped garlic

½ teaspoon soy sauce

½ teaspoon cayenne pepper

Wood: Pecan or other light wood, such as peach

Temperature: Medium-low, direct heat

Rough Cook Time: 5 to 7 minutes

Cooking Equipment: Blender, charcoal grill, small saucepan

Shrimp and Crawfish Étouffée

For me, crawfish, like most freshwater shellfish, don't bring in much flavor on their own. Butter helps a lot, but I want to get even more taste into my étouffée, so I like to add shrimp too. That way I can use the shrimp shells and some blue crabs (usually called gumbo crabs) to make that essence really strong. The other key is to take the time at the start to cook your vegetables down until they almost collapse and become a part of the butter. Now, if you don't have time to make the broth and you want to use only crawfish, you can absolutely do that, and the étouffée will still taste good. But if you have the extra time, I really think the broth helps the flavor.

This is another dish many people believe is a lot harder than it really is. Once you make it, you'll realize that it's much easier and quicker than something like gumbo. Your family and friends will fall in love with it.

Fresh crawfish season in the South usually runs from January through July, but now, thanks to frozen crawfish, you can cook this dish year-round because you can buy frozen peeled crawfish tail meat. I would never use whole frozen crawfish, however, or I'd never be let back onto Bourbon Street ever again.

MAKES 4 TO 6 SERVINGS

2 pounds shell-on shrimp, deveined, shells and tail segments removed and reserved

2 live or frozen blue crabs

10 cups water

3 tablespoons chicken bouillon powder, or as needed

1 cup salted butter, plus 3 tablespoons

1 cup finely chopped yellow onion

½ cup finely chopped green bell pepper

½ cup finely chopped celery

1 tablespoon finely chopped garlic

3 green onions, dark green part only, chopped

⅔ cup all-purpose flour

1½ teaspoons Cajun seasoning

½ teaspoon cayenne pepper

½ teaspoon ground black pepper

In a medium stockpot over high heat, combine the shrimp shells and tail segments, blue crabs, water, and bouillon powder and bring to a boil. Turn the heat to a gentle simmer, cover, and let simmer for 30 minutes.

While the broth simmers, in a large skillet over medium heat, melt the 1 cup butter. Then turn the heat to medium-low and add the yellow onion, bell pepper, celery, garlic, and green onions and cook, stirring frequently, until the vegetables are completely softened and have broken down, about 25 minutes.

Meanwhile, when the broth is ready, remove from the heat, taste for seasoning, and adjust with more bouillon powder if needed. Strain through a fine-mesh sieve, discarding the solids. Set the broth aside.

Back in the large skillet, push the vegetables to the side of the pan. Add the flour, Cajun seasoning, cayenne, and black pepper to the empty side of the pan and cook, stirring regularly, until the flour is nice and toasted, about 4 minutes. Combine the vegetables with the flour mixture and stir to mix thoroughly. Add 5 cups of the broth, a cup or so at a time, stirring constantly to build a gravy. When all the broth is incorporated, cover, turn the heat to low, and simmer the gravy for about 15 minutes. The mixture should have the consistency of a medium-thick gravy.

When the gravy is almost ready, in a medium sauté pan or skillet over medium-high heat, melt the remaining 3 tablespoons butter. Add the shrimp and crawfish meat and cook, stirring frequently, just until they take on color, 3 to 4 minutes.

Using a slotted spoon, transfer the shrimp and crawfish to the gravy and stir to combine. Allow to simmer until just warmed through, 2 to 3 minutes. (I prefer a medium-to-thick gravy for my étouffée, but if it is coming out thicker than you like it, add a little more of the broth.) Taste for seasoning and adjust with bouillon powder if needed.

Serve the étouffée immediately with rice and garnished with the parsley, if desired.

Leftover étouffée will keep in an airtight container in the refrigerator for up to 3 days.

12 ounces frozen shelled crawfish tail meat, thawed

Cooked extra-long-grain white rice for serving

1 pinch dried parsley (optional)

Cooking Equipment: Medium stockpot, large skillet with a lid, medium sauté pan or skillet

Shrimp and Grits

Any time you're boiling or simmering something, it's an opportunity to flavor it with broth instead of just water. So, for shrimp and grits, I use the shells to make a shrimp broth, and I use the broth to cook the grits and make the gravy. If your broth tastes good, you know your gravy will taste good. But the ingredients matter too. Different shrimp taste different, so it's important to find good ones that you like. I love to use Gulf shrimp if I can find them, but any good-quality shell-on shrimp will work.

For this dish, I personally enjoy my gravy a little thicker, but you can make it however you like it. Once you've made the gravy a couple of times, you'll have mastered it, and it'll come really easy.

MAKES 4 SERVINGS

8 slices bacon

2 pounds large shell-on shrimp, deveined, shells and tail segments removed and reserved

4 cups water

4 cups chicken broth

½ cup finely chopped white onion, plus 2 tablespoons

6 garlic cloves, finely chopped

1 tablespoon Cajun seasoning

¼ teaspoon cayenne pepper

2 bay leaves

5 green onions, chopped, keeping white and green parts separate

½ teaspoon granulated onion

½ cup salted butter

2½ tablespoons all-purpose flour

½ teaspoon Kitchen Bouquet

Kosher salt (optional)

SHRIMP GRITS

Reserved shrimp broth

Water as needed

1¼ cups grits (not instant or quick cooking)

1 pinch kosher salt

½ cup salted butter

Cooking Equipment: Large skillet with a lid, large pot, medium saucepan with a lid

Line a large plate with paper towels.

In a large skillet over medium-high heat, cook the bacon in a single layer, flipping the slices about halfway through, until crispy and mahogany colored, 8 to 10 minutes. Once the bacon is crispy, transfer it to the prepared plate to drain and cool, leaving all the fat in the skillet. Remove the skillet from the heat and reserve. When the bacon has cooled, crumble it with your hands or chop it coarsely and set aside.

In a large pot over medium-high heat, combine the reserved shrimp shells and tails, water, chicken broth, ½ cup white onion, garlic, Cajun seasoning, cayenne, bay leaves, and 2 tablespoons of the white parts of the green onions. Stir to mix well and then bring to a simmer. Adjust the heat to maintain a simmer and let simmer, uncovered, for about 40 minutes. Remove from the heat and strain the broth through a fine-mesh sieve; discard the solids. You will need 3½ cups for the gravy, and the remainder is used for the grits.

Return the skillet with the bacon fat to medium-high heat. When the fat is hot, add the shrimp meat and cook, stirring occasionally, until browned but not cooked through, about 3 minutes. Sprinkle the shrimp with the granulated onion, then, using a slotted spoon, transfer the shrimp to a plate and set aside, keeping the bacon fat in the pan.

Set aside 2 tablespoons of the green parts of the green onions and add the remaining green onions (white and green parts) and remaining 2 tablespoons white onion to the skillet and cook, stirring often, until translucent, 2 to 3 minutes. Add the butter and stir until melted, 1 minute or so.

Turn the heat to medium, add the flour to the skillet, and stir to combine. Add the Kitchen Bouquet, mix well, and then stir constantly until the flour has browned further but not burned (the Kitchen Bouquet will turn the flour to brown right away, so you need to allow the color to deepen without scorching), 15 to 20 minutes, depending on your stove.

CONTINUED

Shrimp and Grits, continued

Once the flour is fully browned and no longer tastes floury, add the 3½ cups shrimp broth, about ½ cup at a time, stirring constantly to incorporate before adding more. When all the broth has been incorporated and the mixture is the consistency of a medium-thick gravy, turn the heat to low and simmer very gently, stirring occasionally, for 10 minutes. Taste for seasoning and adjust with salt if needed. Once it is perfect, cover and keep warm over low heat.

To make the grits: Meanwhile, lightly coat the bottom and sides of a medium saucepan with nonstick cooking spray. Measure the remaining shrimp broth and add water as needed to total 5 cups. Pour the liquid into the prepared pan, set over high heat, and bring a boil. Gradually add the grits while stirring constantly, then add the salt. Return the mixture to a boil, then turn the heat to low, cover, and cook, stirring occasionally, until thick and smooth, about 20 minutes. (I like my grits creamy but still with a little texture. You should cook them to the consistency you like, which may call for longer cooking and adding more liquid.) Once the grits are cooked, remove from the heat and stir in the butter until melted. Cover and set aside off the heat. (If you want to time it out so that everything is done around the same time, begin the grits while you are making the gravy.)

Return the gravy to medium heat. Once it is gently simmering, add the crumbled bacon and browned shrimp, turn the heat to low, and simmer until the shrimp are just cooked through, 5 to 10 minutes.

Portion the grits onto individual plates or wide bowls. Top with the shrimp mixture, garnish with the reserved chopped green onion, and serve immediately.

Leftovers will keep in an airtight container in the refrigerator for up to 3 days.

Seafood, Sausage, and Chicken Gumbo

Gumbo takes me back to my mom and her family. That's the Texas-Watts-Compton connection. My mom, the sisters, the aunties, and the great-aunties cooking and talking shit, getting together in the kitchen on Christmas or New Year's, making this magical, majestic pot of oh-my-God. There'd be so many people at the house that I'd get pissed off because I knew I'd only get to have a little bit. We keep our Thanksgiving dinner traditional, but on Christmas and New Year's, I'm all about gumbo.

But remember, the base of that gumbo has to be good. Quit throwing shrimp, crab, sausage, and all that into a broth that tastes like you're eating a dictionary. Get your broth game right. Get your roux game right. You should be able to eat a bowl of that broth with just some French bread and some butter and be happy. Before you put anything in there, you have to taste that roux and taste that broth. I've fired people for not tasting.

I was in a restaurant one time and I had the gumbo, and the shrimp was good and the crab was good. I gave the waitress twenty bucks and said, "Give this to the chef to give to the fisherman," because his broth wasn't shit.

MAKES 6 TO 8 SERVINGS

In a medium stockpot over medium-high heat, combine the water, chicken legs, blue crabs, shrimp shells and tails, bouillon powder, ¾ cup of the yellow onion, garlic cloves, and bay leaves. Bring to a gentle boil and cook, uncovered, until the chicken is cooked through and completely tender, about 1 hour. Using a slotted spoon or tongs, remove the chicken and set aside to cool. Strain the broth and return it to the pot; discard the solids. Season with additional bouillon powder.

Meanwhile, in a large heavy-bottom gumbo pot over medium-low heat, combine the ⅔ cup vegetable oil, flour, and Kitchen Bouquet and, using a high-heat rubber spatula or a wooden spoon, stir almost constantly (with breaks no longer than 2 minutes) until this roux starts to take on somewhat of a peanut butter color, 30 to 45 minutes. Turn the heat to medium and continue stirring almost constantly (with breaks no longer than 30 seconds), until you have a deep chocolate color, 30 to 45 minutes more. Stir in the remaining 1 cup yellow onion, chopped garlic, bell pepper, celery, and green onion and continue stirring until the vegetables have fully wilted and darkened in the roux, about 10 minutes.

CONTINUED

8 quarts water

4 whole chicken legs

4 live or frozen blue crabs

2 pounds large shell-on shrimp, deveined, shells and tail segments removed and reserved

½ cup chicken bouillon powder, or as needed

1¾ cups finely chopped yellow onion

8 garlic cloves, plus 1 tablespoon finely chopped

2 bay leaves

⅔ cup vegetable oil, plus 2 tablespoons

1 cup all-purpose flour

1 teaspoon Kitchen Bouquet

¼ cup finely chopped green bell pepper

1½ tablespoons finely chopped celery

1½ tablespoons finely chopped green onion, white and green parts

Seafood, Sausage, and Chicken Gumbo, continued

In a large skillet over medium-high heat, warm the remaining 2 tablespoons vegetable oil. When the oil is shimmering, add the sausage and brown, stirring occasionally, for about 5 minutes. Using a slotted spoon, transfer the sausage to a bowl. Add the shrimp meat to the skillet and sear for about 2 minutes. Don't worry about cooking the shrimp all the way through, as they will finish cooking in the gumbo. Using the slotted spoon, transfer them to a second bowl. Add about ¼ cup of the broth to the skillet and deglaze, using a wooden spoon to scrape up any browned bits. Pour the contents of the skillet through a fine-mesh sieve into the pot of broth; discard any loose bits.

Add a ladle of broth to the pot of roux, stirring constantly and allowing the broth to incorporate; continue adding broth until you have a medium-thin gravy. Stir in the cayenne, then add the sausage and stir in additional broth until the thickness is the consistency of soup or extremely thin gravy. Cover the pot, lower the heat, and let simmer gently for 1 hour.

Meanwhile, when the chicken is cool enough to handle, pull the meat; discard the skin and bones. Add the chicken meat to the pot, return to a low simmer, and then cover and let simmer for 1 hour more. Adjust the thickness of the gumbo with more broth if you prefer it thinner; taste for seasoning and adjust with more bouillon powder, if needed. Add the crab legs and shrimp meat and return to a gentle simmer, stirring occasionally until the crab legs are warmed through and the shrimp is just cooked, about 2 minutes.

Serve the gumbo over rice, trying to get a little bit of everything in each bowl.

Leftover gumbo will keep in an airtight container in the refrigerator for up to 3 days.

1½ pounds andouille sausage, sliced into ½-inch-thick coins

2 teaspoons cayenne pepper

2 pounds cooked snow crab legs, separated

Cooked extra-long-grain white rice for serving

Cooking Equipment: Medium stockpot; large, heavy-bottom gumbo pot; large skillet

Seafood Boil

Back when I was a kid, I would come out to visit Granny in June, which was pretty much peak crawfish season. She used to make her boils outside in this big, old pot over an open flame. I called it the witches' brew pot.

For this recipe, you can use crawfish, crab, shrimp, or whatever you've got, and since not everybody has an outdoor flame and a huge witches' brew pot like Granny had, I made this a stove-top version. If you're using frozen seafood, thaw it fully before you cook it, either by holding it under cold running water or leaving it in the refrigerator overnight. I always save a little of the broth at the very end of the cook and keep it off to the side to use as a dip for the seafood.

You will see shrimp and crab boil concentrate listed as an ingredient. It is made by companies such as Zatarain's, and a lot of grocery stores carry it. But it is also easy to order online these days if your local store doesn't carry it.

MAKES 8 TO 10 SERVINGS

Fill an extra-large stockpot, with its strainer in place, with the water and bring to a boil over high heat. (If you don't have an insert, you can always use a long-handled strainer to scoop the food out. Just move quickly to avoid overcooking the seafood.) Add the onions, garlic, chiles, shrimp and crab boil concentrate, seafood boil seasoning mix, bouillon powder, menudo spice mix, cayenne, and lemons. Return to a boil and taste for seasoning; it should already taste like a flavorful, spicy broth.

Next, add the potatoes and corn to the pot, cover, and continue boiling until the potatoes are fork-tender and just about fully cooked, about 10 minutes. Add the sausage and butter and return to a boil. Once the butter has melted and the liquid is boiling—about 5 minutes more, depending on the strength of your burner—add the seafood in stages according to size. Huge prawns or lobsters, for instance, need an extra minute or two before you add shrimp, crawfish, crab legs, and the like. Simmer until the seafood is just barely cooked through. This could take anywhere from 2 minutes for small shrimp to 12 minutes or so for a large lobster.

Drain the seafood and vegetables, reserving at least 4 cups of the broth for dipping. Eat immediately with your hands.

Leftover boil and broth will keep in separate airtight containers in the refrigerator for up to 3 days.

13 quarts water

2 large white or yellow onions, quartered

30 garlic cloves

4 serrano chiles, stemmed

1 tablespoon shrimp and crab boil concentrate

¼ cup granulated seafood boil seasoning mix

½ cup chicken bouillon powder

2 tablespoons menudo spice mix

2 tablespoons cayenne pepper

3 lemons, halved

2 pounds petite red potatoes

3 ears corn (or as many as you want), halved crosswise

2 pounds andouille sausage, cut crosswise into thirds

1½ cups salted butter

10 pounds seafood of your choice (such as shell-on shrimp, lobster, crab, live crawfish, and prawns), thawed if frozen

Cooking Equipment: Extra-large stockpot (preferably with a deep strainer insert)

Smoked Crab Legs

To me, the best thing in the world is boiled crab with melted butter. But I also just love to give crab legs a light, quick smoke and eat them with some garlic butter. This smoke is really quick, so you'll have your crab legs ready to go in no time.

MAKES 4 APPETIZER SERVINGS

4 cooked split king crab legs or whole snow crab leg clusters

Creole seasoning for coating

5 tablespoons salted butter

2 tablespoons finely chopped garlic

Wood: Pecan or other light wood such as peach

Temperature: 240°F

Rough Cook Time: About 10 minutes

Cooking Equipment: Smoker, small saucepan (optional)

Follow the instructions in How to Light Your Pit (page 39), aiming for a temperature of 240°F. When the charcoal is ready, add a few chunks of pecan and let the wood burn off for 5 to 10 minutes.

Meanwhile, if using split king crab legs, coat the meat very lightly with Creole seasoning. If using snow crab legs, cut a slit along the legs, then coat along the leg with Creole seasoning, covering it quite well.

In a small saucepan over medium heat, combine the butter and garlic and warm just until melted, then set aside. Or combine the butter and garlic in a small bowl and microwave just until melted.

Load the crab legs into your pit. If using split king crab legs, allow to smoke for about 5 minutes, then brush with some of the garlic butter and continue to smoke for 5 minutes more. If using snow crab legs, just smoke them for 10 minutes.

Take the legs off the pit and eat immediately, with the garlic butter for dipping.

Leftover crab legs will keep in an airtight container in the refrigerator for up to 3 days.

Grilled Crab Legs

Wood: Pecan or other light wood such as peach

Temperature: Medium-low, indirect heat

Rough Cook Time: About 10 minutes

Cooking Equipment: Charcoal grill

You can also smoke the crab legs on a charcoal grill. Set up your grill as instructed in How to Light Your Grill (page 61), aiming for a medium-low, indirect heat. When the charcoal is ready, add a few chunks of pecan. Let the wood burn off for about 5 minutes, then put the grill grate on the grill.

Place the crab legs on the side of the grill away from the charcoal and wood and cover the grill, leaving the vent in the lid above the crab open. If using split king crab legs, brush them with some of the garlic butter after 5 minutes, then smoke for 5 minutes more. If using snow crab legs, just smoke them for 10 minutes. Serve as directed.

Fried Whole Crappie

When Granny would go fishing in the summer, she would always end up frying crappie, buffalo fish, and catfish outdoors in her big, old cast-iron pot over an open flame. The fish were so fresh that their veins popped when they cooked. There was nothing like eating those fish with french fries and a strawberry soda.

There are lots of great freshwater fish in the world, depending on where you are–bream, bluegill, perch, whatever–but crappie is my favorite. It's light and flaky and beautiful. Crappie tastes so good that it pushed fried catfish to the breakfast table in my house. But you can use whatever freshwater fish you've got.

MAKES 4 SERVINGS

In a deep-fryer or a deep, heavy skillet, pour vegetable oil to a depth of about 2 inches, making sure that the crappie will be fully submerged, and heat to 350°F. Set a wire rack on a large baking sheet or line a large plate with paper towels and place near the stove. Put the fish-fry seasoning in a large bowl. You're going to fry in batches, so make sure you're only preparing as many fish as will fit comfortably in your fryer or skillet (most likely one at a time).

Rinse a crappie under cold running water just to moisten and lightly pat dry with a paper or kitchen towel. Dredge in the seasoning, making sure to coat it completely, then shake off any excess seasoning.

Working in batches, gently lay the fish in the hot oil and fry until the crust is golden brown and the fish is floating and crispy, 5 to 6 minutes. Using a skimmer or slotted spatula, transfer the fish to the prepared baking sheet to drain. Continue frying the fish, always allowing the oil to return to 350°F before adding the next batch.

Serve the fish right away, accompanied with hot sauce and white bread.

Leftover fish will keep in an airtight container in the refrigerator for up to 3 days.

Vegetable oil for deep-frying

About 2 cups Fish-Fry Seasoning (page 52)

4 whole crappie (1 to 1½ pounds each), cleaned and head removed

Hot sauce and sliced white bread for serving

Cooking Equipment: Deep-fryer or deep, heavy skillet and deep-frying thermometer

Fried Catfish Fillet

Any time we can fry some goddamn fish, I'm with it. Don't wait until Friday for this one. When I was growing up, we used to eat fried fillets at my Aunt Beulah's in the projects or outside at Granny's in Corsicana, and this just brings me back.

I love to fry up catfish fillets, but you can also use red snapper, almost any kind of perch, whiting, orange roughy, gaspergou, or something like that.

MAKES 4 SERVINGS

Vegetable oil for deep-frying

About 1½ cups Fish-Fry Seasoning (page 52)

4 catfish fillets (6 to 7 ounces each)

Hot sauce for serving

Cooking Equipment: Deep-fryer or deep, heavy skillet and deep-frying thermometer

In a deep-fryer or a deep, heavy skillet, pour vegetable oil to a depth of about 2 inches, making sure that the catfish will be fully submerged, and heat to 350°F. Set a wire rack on a large baking sheet or line a large plate with paper towels and place near the stove. Put the fish-fry seasoning in a large bowl. You're going to fry in batches, so make sure you're only preparing as many fillets as will fit comfortably in your fryer or skillet.

Cut each fillet crosswise into three equal pieces. Rinse the catfish under cold running water just to moisten and lightly pat dry with a paper or kitchen towel. Dredge in the seasoning, making sure to coat it completely, then shake off any excess seasoning.

Working in batches, gently lay the fish in the hot oil and fry until the crust is golden brown, and the filets are floating, and crispy, about 4 minutes. Using a skimmer or slotted spatula, transfer the fish to the prepared baking sheet to drain. Continue frying the fish, always allowing the oil to return to 350°F before adding the next batch.

Serve the catfish right away, accompanied with hot sauce.

Leftover catfish will keep in an airtight container in the refrigerator for up to 3 days.

Blackened Catfish

Always remember that "blackened" is not "burnt." Also, the pan has to be thoroughly greased, because it's horrible when you're trying to make blackened catfish and it falls apart in the pan.

Some people like a sauce on their blackened catfish, but I don't want any sauce on mine. I like the moisture of the fatty catfish sprinkled with spices and cooked in butter and a little bacon fat and that's it. I don't even like it finished with some lemon, but some people do, and that's up to them.

MAKES 4 SERVINGS

4 catfish fillets (6 to 7 ounces each)

About 4 tablespoons Cajun seasoning

2 teaspoons dried rosemary leaves

3 tablespoons salted butter,
or as needed

2 tablespoons rendered bacon fat
(from about 2 slices)

Hot sauce for serving (optional)

Cooking Equipment: Large cast-iron
skillet or your best heavy skillet

Evenly sprinkle each fillet on both sides with 1 tablespoon of the Cajun seasoning. Then evenly sprinkle each fillet on both sides with ½ teaspoon of the rosemary.

Coat a large cast-iron skillet or other heavy skillet with nonstick cooking spray, place over medium-high heat until very hot, and then add the butter and bacon fat and allow them to melt and begin to sizzle. Once sizzling, lay the fillets in the pan, adding only as many as will fit comfortably without overlapping. Let them cook until a nice blackened crust has started to develop on the underside, about 4 minutes, and then, using a spatula, flip the fillets (being careful not to splash the fat on yourself) until blackened on the second side, 2 to 3 minutes more. Using the spatula, transfer the fillets to a plate and repeat with the remaining fillets, adding more butter to the pan as needed.

Serve the catfish right away, accompanied with hot sauce, if desired.

Leftover catfish will keep in an airtight container in the refrigerator for up to 3 days.

Kalin's Fish Tacos

Out here in my little stretch of heaven, I've gotten to meet some new people who also live in the area. How blessed am I to meet John and Kalin Harvard, father-and-daughter entrepreneurs who were opening The Harbor Restaurant in Corsicana during the time I'm calling myself semiretired? So I was able to help them out and consult, and then on some nights we'd all go over to Kalin's house to eat. She's somebody who takes the time to do it right, and she's someone who was very nervous to cook around me at first. But she's such an unbelievable cook.

I've had fish tacos all over, but I had never had a fish taco with crappie, and it was incredible. John makes some good pinto beans, too, so we'd eat these fish tacos with John's pinto beans. I'm very lucky Kalin wanted to share this recipe.

MAKES 4 SERVINGS

JICAMA SLAW

¼ medium or ½ small purple cabbage

¼ medium or ½ small green cabbage

½ medium jicama, peeled

¼ cup mayonnaise

¼ cup Mexican crema

1 tablespoon cider vinegar

Grated zest of 1 lime, plus juice of ½ lime, or as needed

3 green onions, green part only, thinly sliced into 2-inch-long strips

Kosher salt and ground black pepper

FRIED FISH

Peanut oil for deep-frying

¾ cup all-purpose flour

1 teaspoon kosher salt

1 teaspoon ground black pepper

2 eggs

2 cups panko (Japanese bread crumbs)

1½ pounds flaky white fish fillets (such as crappie or tilapia)

To make the slaw: Shred the purple and green cabbage and the jicama into pieces about ¼ inch thick, then pat dry with a paper or kitchen towel.

In a large bowl, combine the mayonnaise, crema, vinegar, and lime zest and stir to incorporate. Add the green onions and lime juice and stir to mix. Season with salt and pepper. This dressing should quite tart and a little salty. Add more lime juice if needed. Add the shredded cabbage and jicama to the dressing and mix thoroughly. Set aside.

To fry the fish: In a deep-fryer or a deep, heavy skillet, pour peanut oil to a depth of 2½ inches and heat to 350°F. Set a wire rack on a large baking sheet or line a large plate with paper towels and place near the stove. Set up your breading station with three wide, shallow bowls. Put the flour into the first bowl, add the salt and pepper, and stir to mix. Crack the eggs into the second bowl and beat lightly. Put the panko into the third bowl.

Pat the fish dry with a paper or kitchen towel and cut into pieces roughly 1 inch wide by 3 inches long. One at a time, dredge the fish pieces in the flour, shaking off any excess, and then dip into the eggs, draining off any excess. Finally, coat each piece completely in the panko and set aside in a single layer (not touching) on a large plate or tray.

Working in batches, gently lay the fish in the hot oil and fry until golden brown and cooked through, about 3 minutes. Using a skimmer or a slotted spoon, transfer to the prepared baking sheet. Continue frying the fish, always allowing the oil to return to 350°F before adding the next batch.

Place a medium skillet over medium-high heat and add enough vegetable oil to heavily coat the bottom of the pan. When the oil is shimmering, add the tortillas, one at a time, and fry, for about 20 seconds on each side, turning once. They should be tender and just starting to crisp around the edges. As the tortillas are ready, stack them on one end of a clean kitchen towel and cover with the other end of the towel to keep warm.

Taste the slaw and adjust the seasoning if needed. Divide the fish evenly among the tortillas. Top with some slaw and a sprinkle of cheese, then fold and serve immediately.

Vegetable oil for deep-frying

8 taco-size corn-flour tortillas (or your preferred tortilla)

Grated Cotija cheese for topping

Cooking Equipment: Deep-fryer or deep, heavy skillet and deep-frying thermometer; medium skillet

THE ROBIN SECTION (MY SIDE-KICKS)

The meats and all that are the stars of the show. The meats are Batman. But you still gotta have a solid Robin to have your back. Your sides gotta be on point too. Collard greens take almost three hours to cook. You gonna cook something for three hours and make it horrible? Hell, no. You gotta make these things right. Sure they're sides, but they're incredible if you do them right.

Potato Salad

First of all, if you don't get your elbows dirty, you aren't making potato salad right. You have to mix it with your hands to make sure all the flavors are mixing in. You also have to taste at every step and season it as you go. And it should taste good every step of the way. Make sure you season the potatoes when they're warm. They need to be warm so you can move the flavor in. First, add the seasoning salt and pepper. Then you taste it. Then you add the mustard and taste it for that tang you want. So while there is an exact recipe here, just know that potato salad has no set recipe. All potatoes are different. If they cook a little too long, they'll have extra moisture and won't need as much relish. If they're a little undercooked, they'll need a little more relish. But don't use too much relish, or you'll soup it out.

I like my potato salad with sweet relish (Del Monte is my favorite). Some people don't like that, but my thing is, do whatever you want, just don't make bad potato salad. Oh and don't forget good mayonnaise. Don't just get Springfield. Have some pride in what you're cooking. Being in Texas now, I like Duke's and Hellmann's. Duke's is some good shit.

MAKES 8 TO 10 SERVINGS

6 pounds russet potatoes, peeled

2 tablespoons seasoning salt

2 teaspoons ground black pepper

¾ cup yellow mustard

2 cups finely diced celery

2 bunches green onions, thickest green part discarded, sliced

10 hard-boiled eggs; 6 peeled and chopped or mashed, 4 halved

3¾ cups sweet relish, or to taste

2½ cups mayonnaise

Sweet paprika for finishing

Chopped fresh parsley for sprinkling

Cooking Equipment: Large pot

In a large pot over high heat, combine the potatoes with water to cover by 2 inches and bring to a boil, then turn the heat to a steady simmer. Some people like the texture of their potato salad to be soft and mashed, and some like it chunky. I like mine with a little of both, so I cook the potatoes until they are tender but not falling apart—until a knife pierces through the center without much resistance—30 minutes to 1 hour, depending on the size of the potatoes.

Drain the potatoes and transfer to a large bowl. Allow to cool until you can handle them easily with your hands. Just make sure they are still warm.

Season the potatoes with the seasoning salt and pepper, tasting as you go. Don't just dump it all in. Then mash the potatoes with a potato masher until they have a varied texture and the seasoning is fully integrated. They should taste good just from the seasoning salt and pepper.

Add the mustard to the potatoes, a little at a time, mixing with your hands and tasting for the desired tartness. Once again, it should almost taste great as is. Then add the celery, green onions, and eggs and mix by hand, getting it all good. Now add the relish. This is the component that makes a wet potato salad versus a dry one. I like my potato salad a little wet. Too much relish and it will be soupy, but too little and it will be like fucking clay. Mix it all the way through. Then add the mayonnaise and mix thoroughly. Finish with the sliced eggs, some paprika, and a sprinkle of parsley on top.

Cover and refrigerate until chilled before serving. It is at its best on the second day but will keep for 1 week. (It shouldn't last that long if it's any good.)

Coleslaw

Coleslaw is a summer favorite. If there's a battle, potato salad always wins and coleslaw is the second choice. But just think, if you bring this coleslaw to the picnic, it'll probably be better than the potato salad somebody else made. I don't love coleslaw on its own, to be honest. But I do love it on a pulled pork sandwich. Sometimes I even sub it onto a Fried Pork Chop Sandwich (page 139).

Coleslaw wilts fast, so it's best to make the dressing in advance and keep it separated from the cabbage until it's time to serve.

MAKES 8 SERVINGS

1 cup plus 3 tablespoons mayonnaise

¼ cup plus 2 tablespoons whole milk

¼ cup cider vinegar

2 tablespoons buttermilk

¼ cup granulated sugar

1 teaspoon kosher salt

½ teaspoon ground black pepper

½ teaspoon celery seed

¼ teaspoon cayenne pepper

¼ teaspoon fresh lemon juice

Two 14-ounce bags shredded cabbage

¼ cup yellow mustard

In a medium bowl, whisk together the mayonnaise, whole milk, vinegar, buttermilk, sugar, salt, black pepper, celery seed, cayenne, and lemon juice until well mixed. If you have time, allow this dressing to sit for at least 15 minutes, or covered and refrigerated for up to 2 days, to allow the flavors to blend before you dress the slaw. But if you don't have the time, the slaw will still be good.

When you're ready to dress the slaw, put the cabbage into a large bowl. Add the mustard and toss to mix thoroughly. Add the dressing and toss again, coating evenly. Taste for seasoning and adjust if needed.

Serve the coleslaw immediately, but it will keep tightly covered in the refrigerator for up to 1 day.

Mashed Potatoes

I love mashed potatoes. There's nothing better than our Smothered Chicken and Gravy (page 132) over some mashed potatoes. But I also think that mashed potatoes need to be good enough to stand on their own without any gravy. I also love them with fried chicken (see page 137). These will make you a hit with your grandkids.

The key to mashed potatoes is to season the potatoes while they're hot and to melt the butter first. I don't even use much milk in mine because I put so much butter in them. But I do sneak in a little bit of powdered ranch seasoning. Also, I don't want big-ass lumps in my potatoes, but you should make yours how you like them.

MAKES 6 TO 8 SERVINGS

In a large pot over high heat, combine the potatoes with water to cover by 2 inches and bring to a boil, then turn the heat to a steady simmer. Cook the potatoes until fork-tender, 20 to 30 minutes.

Drain the potatoes and transfer them to a large bowl. Add the pepper, ranch seasoning, and seasoning salt and mash with a potato masher until the potatoes are at your desired texture. I like mine very smooth. Taste for seasoning and adjust if needed. Add the butter and stir. Then add the milk and stir until completely incorporated. Taste again for seasoning and adjust if needed.

Serve the potatoes immediately, or reheat gently when you're ready to sit down.

Leftover mashed potatoes will keep in an airtight container in the refrigerator for up to 5 days.

4 pounds russet potatoes, peeled

1½ tablespoons ground black pepper

2 teaspoons powdered ranch seasoning

2 teaspoons seasoning salt

¾ cup salted butter, melted

¼ cup whole milk

Cooking Equipment: Large pot

Collard Greens

Any reason to cook a ham hock, for me, is the business, and this is one of the best reasons to do it. Plus, collards is one of the things you judge a Southern home or restaurant on.

Also, when you're going out to church, you get dressed up. You don't go naked. So why would you let your collard greens go out naked? You've got to get dressed up and get fancy with them. That means you've got to build that flavor in your broth first. Collards don't take but 45 minutes to cook, but you've got to take the time to wait on your broth before you get to the greens.

You can make good greens with turkey instead of pork if you prefer, but the taste profile will be different. We make old-fashioned Southern greens with ham hock, and that's what you've got here. You can also swap out the collards for whatever greens you like. I like collards because they stand up longer. Turnip greens and mustard greens taste great; but if you hold them for too long, they get a little bit swampy.

MAKES 6 TO 8 SERVINGS

12 quarts water

2 smoked ham hocks

1 cup chicken bouillon powder

2 banana peppers

½ cup finely chopped yellow onion

12 garlic cloves

10 bunches collard greens, or five 32-ounce bags precut collard greens

1 tablespoon seasoning salt, or as needed

1 tablespoon red pepper flakes, or as needed

1 tablespoon vegetable oil

Cooking Equipment: Large stockpot

In a large stockpot over high heat, combine the water, ham hocks, bouillon powder, banana peppers, onion, and garlic and bring to a rolling boil. Turn the heat to a low boil, cover, and cook until the ham hocks are fully tender, about 2 hours.

Meanwhile, if using bunches of collard greens, strip the leaves from their stems and discard the stems. Working in batches, stack several of the leaves on a cutting board. Grab one edge of the stack, roll it up tightly, and then cut the roll crosswise at 1-inch intervals. You should end up with somewhat long, 1-inch-wide slices. Repeat until all of the greens are sliced. Skip this step if using precut greens.

Fill a large pot or bowl or your sink with water and submerge the greens in the water. Lift the greens from the water, discard the water, and then submerge the greens in two more changes of clean water. Set aside.

Once the ham hocks are tender, add the seasoning salt, then taste for seasoning and adjust if needed. Add the greens and top with the red pepper flakes and vegetable oil. Simmer until the greens are tender but not overcooked, about 45 minutes.

When the greens are ready, pull the ham hocks from the pot, cut or break off the meat, return the meat to the pot, and discard the bones.

Serve the greens, hot, with some of the meat and broth.

Leftover collards will keep in an airtight container in the refrigerator for up to 5 days. Be careful not to overcook the greens or reduce the liquid when reheating.

Brisket Baked Beans

Baked beans are the number-one doctor-up food that you can make. I'd never use canned beans when making pinto beans or anything like that, but I do for baked beans because the work is already done, and it's such an easy thing to add flavor to. You can use any leftover BBQ meat for your beans, but I love them with the flavor of good smoky brisket.

Open the can of beans and drain off and discard about one-fourth of the liquid. Pour the beans and remaining liquid into a large pot, add the mustard, and stir to mix well. The beans should take on a slightly yellow color. Add the brown sugar and mix thoroughly. Taste the beans; you should be able to taste the mustard and brown sugar right away. If you can't taste them, add a little more. Add the onion and brisket and stir. Then add the BBQ sauce and stir again.

Place the pot over medium-low heat, bring to a simmer, and then turn the heat to low. Let simmer gently uncovered, stirring frequently to make sure the beans don't scorch on the bottom of the pot, for 1 hour to blend the flavors. Serve hot or warm.

Leftover beans will keep in an airtight container in the refrigerator for up to 5 days.

MAKES ABOUT 12 SERVINGS

One 117-ounce can baked beans

½ cup yellow mustard, or as needed

1 cup packed dark brown sugar, or as needed

½ cup finely chopped yellow onion

1½ cups chopped smoked brisket, in about ¼-inch pieces

½ cup Bludso's BBQ Sauce (page 54)

Cooking Equipment: Large pot

String Beans with Red Potatoes and Smoked Turkey Necks

String beans are another favorite of mine that my mom would cook on certain holidays, and they were always such a treat. But then sometimes she would cook them on just a regular Wednesday, and they made dinner taste like a holiday meal.

You're not going to cook a whole turkey on a Tuesday, but you can fry some chicken and serve it with these string beans. The truth is, I can't tell if I appreciate these more on a holiday or for a weekday dinner.

MAKES 4 TO 6 SERVINGS

8 quarts water, or as needed

6 meaty smoked turkey necks, or 2 smoked ham hocks

½ cup finely chopped white onion

1 tablespoon finely chopped garlic

2 tablespoons chicken bouillon powder

Seasoning salt

1 pound small-to-medium red potatoes, quartered

2 pounds string beans, stemmed and halved crosswise

1 tablespoon ground black pepper

Cooking Equipment: Large stockpot

In a large stockpot over high heat, combine the water and turkey necks and bring to a rolling boil. Turn the heat to a low boil, cover, and cook for 2 hours.

After the 2 hours, add more water if needed just to cover the necks, then add the onion, garlic, and bouillon powder and stir to combine. Taste for seasoning and add seasoning salt if needed. The liquid should taste like an excellent, slightly salty broth. Add the potatoes and string beans, re-cover, and continue cooking at a low boil until the potatoes are quite tender and the string beans are soft, about 45 minutes. Add the pepper and stir to combine. Taste for seasoning and adjust if needed. Take off heat but leave covered.

Pull the turkey necks from the broth and set them aside just until they are cool enough to handle. Pull the meat from the necks, discarding the skin and bones, and add the meat back to the broth. If you are using ham hocks, you can simply break them up with a cooking spoon in the pot, or remove them, pull the meat, and add it back into the broth; discard the bones and skin.

Serve the string beans and potatoes in bowls along with some of the broth and the meat.

Leftovers will keep in an airtight container in the refrigerator for up to 5 days. Be careful not to overcook the vegetables or reduce the liquid when reheating.

Black-Eyed Peas

Anybody who knows African American culture knows that black-eyed peas are something you've *got* to have on New Year's Day, whether as a side or a main course. (This recipe serves four to six people as an entrée.) They're supposed to bring you good luck for the whole year. But thank God, you can get them year-round.

Chitlins and gumbo are actually huge on New Year's Day too. Usually we have one on Christmas and the other on New Year's. If you have gumbo, you'll always see a little pot of black-eyed peas on the side. But if you're having chitlins, you're definitely going to eat those together with the black-eyed peas.

When you cook this recipe, remember that black-eyed peas look like beans and feel like beans, but they're peas, which means they cook quicker than beans. They are really starchy and cook fast, so you have to stir a lot to make sure you don't let them char up on the bottom of the pot. If they do, you'll have fucked up the whole pot, and there'll be no good luck for you for the whole year.

MAKES 8 TO 10 SERVINGS

In a large stockpot over high heat, combine the water, neck bones, ham hock (if using), bouillon powder, serranos, and bay leaves and bring to a boil. Cover, turn the heat to a simmer, and let simmer until the meat is fall-apart tender, 2 to 3 hours.

When the meat is close to becoming tender, in a large skillet over medium-high heat, warm the vegetable oil. When the oil is shimmering, add the onion, celery, and bell pepper and cook, stirring often, until all the vegetables are wilted, about 6 minutes. Set aside off the heat.

Once the meat is tender, taste the broth and adjust the seasoning with salt and black pepper, if needed. Add the black-eyed peas, vegetable mixture, garlic, chili powder, thyme, and cayenne (if using) and stir well. Return to a simmer, re-cover, and cook, stirring occasionally, until the black-eyed peas are fully tender, 1 to 1½ hours. Keep an eye on the water level throughout the cook and add warm water if needed to maintain the level, being careful not to add too much and dilute the broth. When the black-eyed peas are cooked, taste for seasoning and adjust if needed.

Serve the black-eyed peas in bowls with some of the meat and broth.

Leftover black-eyed peas will keep in an airtight container in the refrigerator for up to 1 week.

4¾ quarts water, or as needed

2 pounds smoked pork neck bones

1 smoked ham hock (optional)

¼ cup chicken bouillon powder

4 serrano chiles, stemmed

2 bay leaves

2 tablespoons vegetable oil

1½ cups finely chopped white onion

1 cup finely chopped celery

1 cup finely chopped green bell pepper

Kosher salt and ground black pepper

2 pounds dried black-eyed peas, rinsed and sorted

¼ cup finely chopped garlic

1 tablespoon dark chili powder

½ teaspoon ground thyme

½ teaspoon cayenne pepper (optional)

Cooking Equipment: Large stockpot, large skillet

Spicy Creole Cabbage

I don't know how it really came about—whether it was leftovers from something or what—I just know that sometimes we would get regular cabbage and sometimes we would get bomb-ass Creole cabbage with leftover ham hocks and sausage and bacon. I'd know when I got home if we were having regular cabbage, because it was cooking in a pot, or Creole cabbage, because it was cooking in a skillet. Sometimes we would have the cabbage as a side and sometimes we would have it as dinner, and that was the whole dinner.

When you go to different parts of the South, you find that everybody cooks Creole cabbage differently. But everyone I know in Texas, or who has Texas roots, cooks it like this.

MAKES 4 TO 6 SERVINGS

1 smoked ham hock

8 slices bacon

1 pound andouille sausage, sliced into ½-inch-thick coins

½ cup finely chopped white onion

3 tablespoons coarsely diced green bell pepper

1 tablespoon finely chopped garlic

1 banana pepper, halved crosswise

1 tablespoon chicken bouillon powder

1 medium head green cabbage, cored and cut into 1-inch dice

2¼ cups water

3 tablespoons salted butter

1 tablespoon Cajun seasoning

1 teaspoon cayenne pepper

Cooking Equipment: Medium pot with a lid, large skillet with a lid or a Dutch oven

In a medium pot over high heat, combine the ham hock with water to cover by several inches and bring to a boil. Cover and continue to boil until the ham hock is soft enough to cut easily with a knife but not completely falling apart, about 2 hours. Transfer the ham hock to a plate and discard the water.

Meanwhile, in a large skillet or Dutch oven over medium heat, cook the bacon in a single layer, turning occasionally, until somewhat browned and most of the fat is rendered, about 6 minutes. Add the andouille, turn the heat to medium-high, and cook, stirring the bacon and andouille together, until the andouille has started to brown and the bacon is fully cooked but not overly crispy, 3 to 4 minutes more. Using a slotted spoon or spatula, transfer the bacon and andouille to a plate.

Add the onion, bell pepper, garlic, and banana pepper to the fat remaining in the pan, turn the heat to medium, and cook, stirring, for about 2 minutes. Stir in the bouillon powder, then add the cabbage, 2¼ cups water, and butter and stir to mix thoroughly. Cover, adjust the heat to maintain a simmer, and cook, stirring occasionally, until the cabbage begins to wilt, 5 to 10 minutes.

While the cabbage is cooking, slice the meat off the cooled ham hock and discard any large chunks of fat and the bone. Roughly chop the meat. Then, coarsely chop the cooled bacon or crumble it with your hands.

Once the cabbage has wilted a bit, add the bacon, andouille, ham hock meat, Cajun seasoning, and cayenne and stir to combine. Cover and continue to simmer, stirring occasionally, until the cabbage is completely tender, 10 to 15 minutes more. Taste for seasoning and adjust if needed.

Serve the cabbage, along with the meat and some of the broth, in bowls.

Leftovers will keep in an airtight container in the refrigerator for up to 5 days.

Down-Home Mac and Cheese

Who the hell doesn't like mac and cheese? Especially when it's done right—Southern style. This mac and cheese is gonna put some goddamn South in your mouth. Whoever makes this on a Wednesday night, you're gonna swear you're having Sunday dinner with the pastor in the house.

I've had so many mac and cheeses with so many different kinds of cheese. But we basically wanted you to be able to have a great one without getting too complicated. And please, please season your noodles *after* you boil them.

MAKES 6 TO 8 SERVINGS

Kosher salt

¾ cup unsalted butter,
plus 3 tablespoons

5 tablespoons all-purpose flour

2 teaspoons ground black pepper,
plus 1½ tablespoons

2 teaspoons garlic salt,
plus 1½ tablespoons

½ teaspoon mustard powder

¼ teaspoon cayenne pepper

1½ cups whole milk

¾ cup half-and-half

2¼ cups shredded extra-sharp
cheddar cheese

2 cups shredded medium-sharp
cheddar cheese

1½ cups shredded
Monterey Jack cheese

1 pound small elbow macaroni

Cooking Equipment: 9 by 13-inch
baking dish, 2 medium pots

Preheat the oven to 400°F. Lightly coat a 9 by 13-inch baking dish with nonstick cooking spray.

Fill a medium pot with water, bring to a boil over high heat, and add a pinch of salt.

In a second medium pot over medium-low heat, melt the ¾ cup butter. Add the flour, 2 teaspoons black pepper, 2 teaspoons garlic salt, mustard powder, and cayenne and whisk constantly until all the ingredients are incorporated and the flour no longer tastes floury, about 2 minutes. Whisking constantly, very slowly drizzle in the milk and ½ cup of the half-and-half, continuing to whisk until the liquid is fully incorporated and the mixture begins to bubble gently.

Continue to cook, stirring constantly, until the mixture has thickened just enough to fully coat the back of a spoon, about 4 minutes. (Be very careful not to scorch the milk or the dish will have a bitter, burned flavor.) Remove from the heat; add all the extra-sharp cheddar, 1¼ cups of the medium cheddar, and ½ cup of the Monterey Jack; and stir until the cheeses have melted.

Meanwhile, add the macaroni to the boiling water and cook until al dente, about 1 minute less than the package-recommended cooking time. Drain the macaroni and transfer to a large bowl. Add the remaining 3 tablespoons butter and 1½ tablespoons each black pepper and garlic salt and mix well.

Add the cheese sauce to the seasoned macaroni and mix thoroughly. Transfer the macaroni mixture to the prepared baking dish and level the surface. Sprinkle evenly with the remaining ¾ cup medium cheddar and 1 cup Monterey Jack.

Bake until the sauce is bubbling and the top is golden brown, about 15 minutes. Serve hot or warm.

Leftover mac and cheese will keep in an airtight container in the refrigerator for up to 5 days.

Cornbread

You can eat cornbread with beans, greens, chili—with everything. It might be the greatest sidekick of all. What *can't* you eat cornbread with? You can even use it to make my Cornbread Dressing (page 237). It's so fast and so simple.

I remember, one time, Granny made dinner and everybody sat down. But then she realized she had forgotten the cornbread, so she made everybody get up from the table until she made it. It's just that important a part of the meal.

Preheat the oven to 400°F. Thoroughly grease a 9 by 13-inch baking dish with vegetable shortening (I prefer butter-flavored Crisco).

In a large bowl, combine the cornmeal, flour, sugar, baking soda, baking powder, and salt and stir to mix thoroughly.

In a medium bowl, whisk together the buttermilk and egg yolks until well blended. Add the buttermilk mixture to the cornmeal mixture and whisk until fully incorporated. Then, beat the egg whites until stiff. Add the butter, vegetable oil, and egg whites to the buttermilk mixture and mix again. Pour the mixture into the prepared baking dish.

Bake until cooked through and golden brown, 30 to 40 minutes. When the center is solid to the touch, it's right; but you can also stab it with a toothpick, if it comes out clean your cornbread is cooked.

As soon as the cornbread is out of the oven, brush the top with more melted butter, then cut into twelve squares. Serve immediately.

Leftover cornbread will keep, tightly covered, in the refrigerator for up to 5 days.

MAKES 8 TO 12 SERVINGS

1 cup enriched yellow cornmeal

1 cup all-purpose flour

1 tablespoon granulated sugar

1 teaspoon baking soda

1 teaspoon baking powder

½ teaspoon kosher salt

2 cups buttermilk

2 eggs, separated

½ cup salted butter, melted and cooled, plus more for finishing

2 teaspoons vegetable oil

Cooking Equipment: 9 by 13-inch baking dish

THE BEGINNING OF A BEAUTIFUL DAY

You've got a long day of BBQ ahead of you. If you're gonna be cooking a brisket for fourteen hours, you'd better start your day off right with a good-ass breakfast. How you start is how you finish, so if you begin with a hell of a good breakfast, you'll end it with a hell of a good brisket.

I grew up on catfish and eggs, and grits and eggs. This whole chapter is filled with stuff you can mix and match from other sections. Fry up a pork chop, some chicken wings, or a catfish; cook some eggs or grits; make some gravy, and you can turn the most important meal of the day into the most important meal of the year.

Perfect Grits

The truth is, if you read the grits box, you'll cook your grits perfectly, but you can enhance them. I like really buttery grits (I use a whole stick), but the amount of butter is up to you. Just keep in mind that grits should taste good all by themselves, and that's really just about using enough salt and butter.

I don't like quick-cooking or instant grits. Anything good takes time. I take pride in my grits.

MAKES 4 SERVINGS

4 cups water (or according to package instructions)

1 cup grits (not instant or quick cooking)

Kosher salt

4 to 8 tablespoons salted butter

Cooking Equipment: Medium saucepan

Lightly coat the bottom and sides of a medium saucepan with nonstick cooking spray, pour in the water, and bring to a boil over high heat. Gradually add the grits while stirring constantly, then add 1 pinch salt. Return the mixture to a boil, then turn the heat to low, cover, and cook, stirring occasionally, until thick and smooth, about 20 minutes. I like my grits creamy but still with a little texture. You should cook them to the consistency you like, which may call for longer cooking and adding more liquid.

When the grits are ready, remove from the heat and stir in as much of the butter as you like. Taste and adjust the seasoning with salt, if needed.

Grits are best when eaten right away.

Spicy Maple Breakfast Sausage

I love maple sausage, and I love spicy breakfast sausage. This is both. To me, eggs are eggs and grits are grits. The meat has gotta be what stands out. I want a spicy, good-tasting, memorable sausage, and this is that sausage.

MAKES 6 TO 8 SERVINGS

If you are grinding the pork, put it in the freezer for about 45 minutes to firm up a little before you grind it. Then fit your grinder with the coarse-grind plate and grind the pork shoulder and pork belly.

In a large bowl, combine the maple sugar, red pepper flakes, salt, sage, black pepper, cloves, fennel seed, and marjoram and mix thoroughly, making sure to break up any clumps of sugar. Add the pork and ice water and mix until the meat is evenly incorporated with the seasoning. Cover and refrigerate for up to 3 days (or freeze for up to 4 months).

Just before you're ready to cook, loosely shape the sausage mixture into patties about 1 inch thick; or whatever size you prefer—like you are making burgers. I like a big sausage patty, so I make mine about 3 ounces each. Don't pack the meat tightly.

Set a large cast-iron (ideally) or nonstick skillet over medium-high heat, then coat lightly with vegetable oil. Working in batches, add the patties and fry, turning once, until crispy and golden brown with a touch of blackening and just barely cooked through, about 3 minutes on each side. If they are beginning to blacken too quickly, lower the heat. And don't press down on them, you son of a bitch. You want to keep these things juicy. Transfer to a plate and keep warm. Repeat with the remaining patties, adding more oil to the pan as needed.

Serve the sausage immediately.

2 pounds boneless pork shoulder, cut into 1-inch cubes (see Note)

8 ounces pork belly, cut into 1-inch cubes, or an additional 8 ounces boneless pork shoulder

3 tablespoons maple sugar, or 2 tablespoons packed dark brown sugar

2 tablespoons red pepper flakes

1 tablespoon plus 2 teaspoons kosher salt

2 teaspoons ground sage

1 teaspoon ground black pepper

½ teaspoon ground cloves

½ teaspoon fennel seed

¼ teaspoon ground marjoram

1 tablespoon ice water

Vegetable oil for frying

Cooking Equipment: Meat grinder (optional), large cast-iron or nonstick skillet

Note: If you don't have a meat grinder, or you don't want to break it out, you can buy 2½ pounds coarsely ground pork that has a good amount of fat.

Bacon and Sausage Gravy with Biscuits

Biscuits and gravy was something my granny used to make. It was a staple at her house, and she'd always say, "Don't skimp on the bacon or the sausage, goddamnit." Have this with a couple eggs, and that's breakfast.

You can use any biscuits that you like, though I prefer a soft, flaky buttermilk biscuit. Honestly I'm not a baker, so I just use Pillsbury Flaky Buttermilk biscuits. The main thing is the gravy, and using milk instead of water and a lot of black pepper. Sometimes I just use sausage. Sometimes I just use bacon. I feel like doing both here.

MAKES 4 SERVINGS

10 ounces bulk spicy pork sausage (see page 207)

8 slices bacon

¼ cup all-purpose flour

1¼ teaspoons chicken bouillon powder

Ground black pepper

2 cups whole milk, or as needed

Kosher salt (optional)

4 large biscuits

3 tablespoons salted butter, melted

Cooking Equipment: Medium skillet, large skillet

Lightly coat a medium skillet with nonstick cooking spray and set over medium-high heat. When the skillet is hot, add the sausage and cook, stirring or turning over often, until browned and just cooked through, 4 to 6 minutes. Remove from the heat and let cool.

Lightly coat a large skillet with nonstick cooking spray and set over medium to medium-high heat. Lay the bacon in a single layer in the skillet and cook, flipping once, until browned, about 3 minutes on each side. Be very careful not to burn the bacon or the bacon fat or it will turn your gravy dark. If you are nervous about it, take your time and cook the bacon low and slow for 4 to 5 minutes on each side. (I've messed this part up so many times by being in a hurry.) Once the bacon is cooked, transfer it to a plate, leaving the fat behind in the pan.

Turn the heat to medium-low; add the flour, bouillon powder, and ½ teaspoon pepper to the bacon fat; and whisk constantly until the flour just begins to brown and no longer tastes floury, about 2 minutes. Add the milk, ½ cup or so at a time, whisking constantly to incorporate after each addition. When all the milk is incorporated, continue to whisk until thickened to your desired consistency, about 4 minutes for a fairly thick gravy.

Crumble the cooled bacon and sausage with your hands, stir into the gravy, turn the heat to medium, and warm through, about 1 minute. Taste for seasoning and adjust with salt and black pepper, if needed. If your gravy is too thick, you can stir in a few tablespoons milk to thin it. If you want the gravy thicker, you can continue to simmer it over low heat to reduce.

When ready to serve, brush the tops of the biscuits with the butter, then split the biscuits open and pour the gravy over the tops, or, if you like, put the gravy in the middle, like a sandwich.

Leftover gravy will keep in an airtight container in the refrigerator for up to 3 days.

Buttermilk Pancakes

Do you add pancakes to your bath? Then why are you adding water to your pancakes? Adding water to your pancakes should be right up there with cheating on your wife.

This is a family recipe we used to do. I know there are some good pancake box mixes that I enjoyed in the past, but when my mom would make these pancakes, they were the best in the world. I love light, fluffy pancakes. And burn them edges, goddamnit.

In a large bowl, combine the flour, sugar, baking powder, baking soda, and salt and stir to mix well.

In a medium bowl, whisk together the buttermilk, butter, egg yolks, and vanilla until thoroughly blended. Add the buttermilk mixture to the flour mixture and whisk until thoroughly combined. Set aside to rest for at least 15 minutes, or for up to 2 hours.

When it is time to cook the pancakes, if using an electric griddle, preheat to 350°F. If using a stove-top griddle or skillet, set over medium-high heat.

Meanwhile, in a medium bowl, whisk the egg whites to soft peaks. Using a rubber spatula, gently but thoroughly fold the egg whites into the batter, trying to deflate the whites as little as possible.

Lightly coat the griddle or pan with nonstick cooking spray, ladle on ½ cup of the batter, and cook until bubbles appear on the surface, the underside is golden brown, and the edges are crispy but not burned, 2 to 3 minutes. Then flip the pancake and cook until the second side is golden brown, 2 to 3 minutes more. Transfer to a plate. This is your test pancake, if the bottom browned too quickly or remained too pale once the pancake was cooked, adjust the temperature as needed. Repeat with the remaining batter, coating the griddle or pan with more cooking spray as needed.

Serve the pancakes topped with melted butter and maple syrup. They are best when eaten immediately.

MAKES 4 SERVINGS

2 cups all-purpose flour

3 tablespoons granulated sugar

½ teaspoon baking powder

½ teaspoon baking soda

½ teaspoon kosher salt

2 cups buttermilk

½ cup salted butter, melted and cooled, plus more for serving

2 eggs, separated

1½ teaspoons vanilla extract

Maple syrup for serving

Cooking Equipment: Large griddle, nonstick skillet, or your favorite skillet for pancakes

Noah's Chorizo and Smoked Potato Breakfast Burritos

This is an at-home version of the breakfast burrito that Noah made for Cofax Coffee in Los Angeles. The potatoes and tomatillos take on smoke flavor, which infuses the whole burrito. It's really popular as a vegetarian burrito, too, just by going heavier on the potatoes and leaving out the chorizo. The hash also tastes great on its own or with some eggs and tortillas.

If you don't have a way to blacken the poblanos—or don't want to—you can substitute a red and a green bell pepper, seeded and diced, and cook them long enough with the onion to soften fully. The temperature is ideal up around 285°F, but they're really just meant to be thrown into the pit with whatever else is cooking.

You can make the hash and the salsa in advance and then heat it all up in the morning for breakfast.

MAKES 6 TO 8 SERVINGS

1 pound russet potatoes

Vegetable oil for coating,
plus 5 tablespoons, or as needed

Kosher salt

Ground black pepper

2 pounds tomatillos, husks
removed, rinsed

3 poblano chiles

3 árbol chiles, stemmed

2 garlic cloves

2½ pounds Mexican chorizo,
casing removed

1 cup diced white onion

8 eggs

6 extra-large flour tortillas, or 8 large
flour tortillas

3 cups shredded sharp cheddar
cheese or blend of sharp cheddar
and Monterey Jack

½ cup Pico de Gallo (see page 108)

Pierce each potato five or six times with the tines of a fork. Lightly coat the potatoes with vegetable oil and season liberally with salt and pepper. Lightly coat the tomatillos with vegetable oil, season with salt, and place on a small baking sheet to catch any dripping juices during cooking.

Follow the instructions on How to Light Your Pit (page 39), aiming for a temperature of 285°F. When the charcoal is ready, add two or three chunks of pecan and let the wood burn off for 5 to 10 minutes.

Put the potatoes directly on the racks in your pit and set the pan of tomatillos in the pit, then watch your temperature. Any time it drops below 285°F, add a little more wood and charcoal.

Smoke the tomatillos and potatoes for about 1 hour. The potatoes will have darkened from the smoke and softened a bit, and tomatillos should be soft, like water balloons, and have turned a deep, khaki green.

Meanwhile, place the poblanos, one at a time, directly over a gas-stove burner on high heat, turning them with tongs until they are evenly blackened all over, or on a baking sheet under a preheated broiler, again turning as needed until evenly blackened all over. (Or in a pinch, you can even throw them right onto the coals of your pit.) Transfer the poblanos to a bowl, cover with aluminum foil or plastic wrap, and let steam for about 5 minutes. When cool enough to handle, peel the poblanos, remove the stems and seeds (do not rinse the poblanos, or they will lose a lot of their flavor), dice them, and set aside.

When the potatoes and tomatillos are ready, pull them out of the pit. Set the potatoes aside until they are cool enough to handle. Transfer the tomatillos to a stand blender or to a large bowl if using an immersion blender. Place a

CONTINUED

Noah's Chorizo and Smoked Potato Breakfast Burritos, continued

Wood: Pecan

Temperature: 285°F

Rough Cook Time: About 1 hour

Cooking Equipment: Baking sheet(s), smoker, stand or immersion blender, small skillet, large skillet, stove-top griddle or large nonstick skillet

small skillet over medium-high heat and add 1 tablespoon of the vegetable oil, the árbol chiles, and garlic and fry, stirring frequently, until the garlic is lightly browned and the chiles are toasted but not burned, about 1 minute. Transfer the contents of the skillet to the blender or bowl, season aggressively with salt, and blend until smooth. Taste for seasoning and adjust, if needed. This salsa should be smoky, acidic, spicy, and salty. Set aside to cool.

When the potatoes are cool enough to handle, dice them into about ½-inch pieces. They should be softer than raw yet not completely cooked. But if they are fully cooked, that's okay too.

Now, in a large skillet over medium-high heat, warm 2 tablespoons vegetable oil. Add the chorizo and cook, stirring frequently and allowing it to crumble apart, until cooked through and tender. Depending on the coarseness of the grind, it can take anywhere from 5 to 10 minutes to cook. Using a slotted spoon, transfer the chorizo to a bowl and set aside.

Pour off all but 2 tablespoons of the chorizo fat from the pan and return the skillet to medium-high heat. Add the onion and poblanos, season with salt, and cook, stirring often, until softened, 3 to 4 minutes. Add the potatoes, season with salt and pepper, stir well, and then cook, stirring frequently, until cooked through and soft. The timing will depend on how cooked the potatoes were when they came out of the pit. Return the chorizo to the pan and stir until fully combined and warmed through. Remove from the heat and stir in ¾ cup of the salsa. Taste for seasoning and adjust if needed.

Set a stove-top griddle or large nonstick skillet over medium heat.

Meanwhile, cook the eggs to your liking. I like a soft scramble, but any preparation will work. Mix the eggs into the potato-chorizo hash.

One at a time, warm the tortillas on the griddle or in the skillet just until they are pliable and easy to roll, about 30 seconds on each side. As the tortillas are ready, stack them on one end of a clean kitchen towel and cover with the other end of the towel to keep warm.

Lay the tortillas flat on a work surface. Divide the cheese evenly across all the tortillas. Next, add the hash, dividing it evenly. Then top the hash with a couple spoonfuls of the pico de gallo. Fold in the sides, then fold up the bottom and roll up.

Return the griddle to medium heat and add about 1 tablespoon vegetable oil. When the oil is hot, add two burritos, seam-side down, and cook until crunchy and golden on the underside. Then flip them and cook until crunchy and golden on the second side. Repeat with the remaining burritos, adding more oil as needed.

Serve the burritos immediately, with the remaining tomatillo salsa alongside.

Leftover hash and salsa will keep in separate airtight containers in the refrigerator for up to 6 days.

Fried Pork Chop, Catfish, or Chicken Wings and Eggs

Like I always say, especially when you've got a long day of smoking, you want a good breakfast. And I like a twist on breakfast. Chicken wings or pork chops or fresh-caught fish from that morning — I love any of these with some sausage and with my eggs over easy so I can break them up in my grits.

Salted butter

Eggs

Small chicken wings, fried as directed in Fried Chicken (page 137)

Bone-in pork chops, fried as directed in Fried Pork Chop Sandwich (page 139)

Catfish fillets, fried as directed in Fried Catfish Fillet (page 172)

In a deep, heavy skillet over medium heat, melt the butter. Add however many eggs you'd like and cook to your desired style. Serve with your meat of choice and any of the other breakfast dishes in this chapter.

THAT SPECIAL TIME OF YEAR

The holidays—come on now. People are different around Thanksgiving and Christmas. It's just a different time of year. As Granny would say, "If I only get it one time a year where it seems like the whole world is nice, I'll take it." These holidays revolve around family and food, so it's the time to get everybody together. The night before Thanksgiving is one of the most fun nights of the year, with everyone off work and in the kitchen talking and cooking and eating. Then you're all up in the morning, and the pit is getting lit and it's the same thing—even if Aunt Ethel brings her nasty-ass Jell-O mold, which for some reason still tastes good around the holidays.

The holidays are not just about food, they are about people too. So take time to enjoy your loved ones, because when you look around the table the next time, they might not be there. Cherish every moment.

Smoked Turkey Breast

There are times when it might not be Thanksgiving but you still want turkey. The cool thing is, if you know your pit, you can get incredible smoked turkey breast off of it in about three hours. It's a quick, delicious smoke. Or if you're cooking for a smaller number of people on Thanksgiving and don't want to do a whole turkey, this recipe will get you some delicious turkey on the table that, by the time it comes out of the pit, tastes like a Southern ham.

Some people like a wet brine on their turkey breast, but I prefer a dry rub.

One 9- to 10-pound, skin-on, bone-in whole turkey breast

½ recipe Butter Mixture (page 224)

About 1 cup Bludso's Brisket Rub (page 48)

Apple juice for spraying

4 tablespoons salted butter, melted

Wood: Hickory, pecan, and apple

Temperature: 240° to 250°F

Rough Cook Time: About 3 hours

Cooking Equipment: Smoker, small saucepan, meat injector, spray bottle, instant-read thermometer

Choosing and Prepping a Turkey Breast

I like the whole breast, with the bone in and skin attached. Just don't get one that's all beat up or anything. The skin looks all pretty and mahogany colored when it has finished smoking, plus it gives you extra flavor and protects the top layer of that meat from getting dried out.

Seasoning Your Turkey Breast

When you're ready to inject, dry off the turkey breast with a paper or kitchen towel. Then fill the injector with some of the butter mixture and inject the breast, using a 1-ounce injection each time. First, inject one half breast three times, trying to inject in three different areas of the breast but always working from the same hole (so you don't keep breaking open different parts of the skin). Pushing the needle through the center of the breast for each injection, angle the needle toward a different area of the breast each time, so you're injecting the right side, then the left side, and then the middle. Go toward the back of each area with the needle, continuing to inject as you pull the needle slowly out of the breast. Repeat on the other half breast.

Next, season the whole breast with a nice even layer of the rub. Turkey can take a lot of pepper, which gives it a nice Southern flair.

Smoking Your Turkey Breast

Follow the instructions in How to Light Your Pit (page 39), aiming for a temperature of 250°F. When the charcoal is ready, start with about 70 percent hickory and 30 percent pecan. Let the wood burn off for 5 to 10 minutes.

Now load the turkey breast onto the rack in your pit and then keep an eye on the temperature. Every time the temperature drops to 240°F, add a little more wood and charcoal. After the first load, you're adding pecan and a little applewood. Then after about 2½ hours, it's pecan and charcoal the rest of the way. You want that heavy hickory smoke only at the beginning.

Once the seasoning starts to adhere—after about 1 hour—start spraying the breast with apple juice every time you open your pit to check the breast or the wood. With the bone in, you need to go until the internal temperature of the breast reaches 160°F on an instant-read thermometer.

Once the turkey breast is cooked, baste it with the melted butter just before it comes out of the pit and then let rest for at least 30 minutes, though 1 hour is ideal, before carving.

Carving Your Turkey Breast

Using a sharp knife, either slice directly off the side of the breast, or cut each breast half off the breastbone and slice crosswise into thin slices.

Leftover turkey breast will keep tightly covered in the refrigerator for up to 6 days.

Smoked Turkey

The history of this recipe for my family is going over to my Unc's in Watts when I was growing up; that smell of turkey coming off the pit, really gets me. Then Granny would always tell me, "You want the pit cleaned out and the wood all loaded the night before so you can hit the ground running in the morning."

People think smoking turkey is hard, but it's not. Some people like their poultry smoked fast, and you can do that on poultry and it'll work, but I still like mine low and slow. I like a deep, hickory smoke– I want the bone on my turkey to be smoked. I've had people try my turkey and say, "Oh wait, I don't eat pork," and that's the truth.

Turkey is the only meat that we inject in this book. That's because it's so big and has so little fat. I like to use a mixture of melted butter, water, and chicken bouillon powder.

One 14- to 16-pound turkey

BUTTER MIXTURE

1 cup salted butter

1 cup water

1 tablespoon chicken bouillon powder, or as needed

Garlic salt

Ground black pepper

Apple juice for spraying

4 tablespoons salted butter, melted

Wood: Hickory, pecan, and apple

Temperature: 240° to 250°F

Rough Cook Time: 5 to 7 hours (This really depends on the size of the bird.)

Cooking Equipment: Kitchen twine (optional), small saucepan, meat injector, smoker, spray bottle, instant-read thermometer

Choosing and Prepping a Turkey

Look for a fresh turkey that has some nice skin on it and isn't too beat up. Make sure you remove any neck bones or giblets from the body cavity (they can be reserved for Thanksgiving Broth, page 239). Keep the little high-heat plastic fastener, if it has one, attached to the legs. If it doesn't have that little fastener, trussing the legs together with kitchen twine will make for a much better-looking turkey, but you can skip this step.

Seasoning Your Turkey

To make the butter mixture: In a small saucepan over medium heat, combine the butter, water, and bouillon powder and warm just until the butter has melted. Remove from the heat, taste for seasoning, and adjust with additional bouillon powder, if needed. Transfer to a tall, narrow container (so it's easier to fill the injector) and let cool to room temperature. Be careful not to let it sit so long it stiffens up. (This is probably more than you will need, but I like to make a big batch just in case it spills out during the injecting.)

When you're ready to inject, dry off the turkey with a paper or kitchen towel. Then fill the injector with some of the butter mixture and inject the turkey, using a 1-ounce injection each time. First, inject one half breast three times, trying to inject in three different areas of the breast but always working from the same hole (so you don't keep breaking open different parts of the skin). Pushing the needle through the center of the breast for each injection, angle the needle toward a different area of the breast each time, so you're injecting the right side, then the left side, and then the middle. Go toward the back of each area with the needle, continuing to inject as you pull the needle slowly out of the breast. After injecting both breast halves, inject 1 ounce of the mixture into each thigh.

CONTINUED

Smoked Turkey, continued

Next, season the turkey very liberally with garlic salt and pepper. Tuck the wings behind the bird. Set aside at room temperature for at least 1 hour or in the refrigerator for up to 24 hours before cooking.

Smoking Your Turkey

Follow the instructions in How to Light Your Pit (page 39), aiming for a temperature of 250°F. When the charcoal is ready, start with about 70 percent hickory and 30 percent pecan. Let the wood burn off for 5 to 10 minutes.

Now load the turkey, breast-side up onto the rack in your pit and then keep an eye on the temperature. Every time the temperature drops to 240°F, add a little more wood and charcoal.

After 2 hours, open the pit and spray the turkey with apple juice. After 3 hours, add a small applewood chunk to the firebox. From then on, it's pecan and charcoal the rest of the way. Continue smoking, spraying with apple juice every time you open the pit to check the turkey or the wood. At 4 hours, check the internal temperature of the thigh with an instant-read thermometer. (The thigh is cooked at 165°F and the breast is cooked at 150°F.) Continue smoking, being careful not to overcook the turkey and dry it out.

Once the turkey is cooked, baste it with the melted butter just before it comes out of the pit and then let rest for at least 30 minutes, though 1 hour is ideal, before carving.

Carving Your Turkey

Using a sharp knife, separate the leg quarters from the breast and then cut down between the drumsticks and thighs (the drumstick is a trophy and ready to serve), separating them into individual pieces. Separate the thigh meat from the bone and then cut it into slices, discarding the bone. Next, slice the turkey breast from the side, cutting into thin serving slices. Alternately, you can remove the breast halves from the breast bones and slice them crosswise.

Leftover turkey will keep, tightly covered, in the refrigerator for up to 6 days.

Fried Turkey

This is one that my granny used to do in her big old witches' brew pot. Fried turkeys started getting popular in the mid-1990s, but we've been doing them forever.

Fried turkey is all about the injection. We used to eat fried, roasted, *and* smoked turkeys on holidays, since everybody has a different preference. I don't know which one is my favorite, but if I had to pick, I'd probably say it's fried.

It's important to get your timing right. If you're eating at six o'clock, you don't want to drop your turkey until five. Otherwise, it will get all soggy and that butter will be leaking out before you cut it. This should be the last thing you cook on Thanksgiving.

If you've never fried a turkey before, please test it out before you do it for Thanksgiving.

Choosing and Prepping a Turkey and Your Fryer

Look for a fresh turkey that has some nice skin on it and isn't too beat up. Make sure you remove any neck bones or giblets from the body cavity (they can be reserved for Thanksgiving Broth, page 239). Keep the little high-heat plastic fastener, if it has one, attached to the legs. If it doesn't have that little fastener, trussing the legs together with kitchen twine will make for a much better-looking turkey, but you can skip this step.

If you are not familiar with your outdoor turkey fryer setup, please be extra careful and follow all the safety guidelines. Some fryers will have a fill-to line for oil based on the weight of the turkey. But the safest way to know how much oil you need is to put the raw turkey in the pot (I do it while it's still in the packaging) and then add water to the pot to cover the turkey by about 2 inches. You should have several inches of space between the water line and the rim of the pot. If you don't, the pot is not big enough. Remove the turkey from the pot and mark the water line with a piece of tape. Make sure to dry the pot completely before adding the oil.

Seasoning Your Turkey

To make the butter mixture: In a small saucepan over medium-low heat; combine the water, onion, garlic, and bouillon powder; bring just to a simmer; and let barely simmer for about 15 minutes. Remove from heat; add the butter, Creole seasoning, and cayenne; and let stand until the butter melts fully. Strain the mixture through a fine-mesh sieve into any tall, narrow container (so it's easier to fill the injector) and let cool to room temperature. Be careful not to let it sit so long it stiffens up.

CONTINUED

One 14- to 16-pound turkey

CREOLE BUTTER MIXTURE

2 cups water

1 tablespoon finely chopped yellow onion

1½ teaspoons finely chopped garlic

2 tablespoons chicken bouillon powder

1 cup unsalted butter, at room temperature

1 teaspoon Creole seasoning

1 teaspoon cayenne pepper

Creole seasoning for seasoning

Ground black pepper

Peanut oil for deep-frying

Cooking Equipment: Kitchen twine (optional), outdoor turkey fryer, small saucepan, meat injector, deep-frying thermometer, instant-read thermometer

Fried Turkey, continued

When you're ready to inject, dry off the turkey with a paper or kitchen towel. Then fill the injector with some of the butter mixture and inject the turkey, using a 1-ounce injection each time. First, inject one half breast three times, trying to inject in three different areas of the breast but always working from the same hole (so you don't keep breaking open different parts of the skin). Pushing the needle through the center of the breast for each injection, angle the needle toward a different area of the breast each time, so you're injecting the right side, then the left side, and then the middle. Go toward the back of each area with the needle, continuing to inject as you pull the needle slowly out of the breast. After injecting both breast halves, inject 1 ounce of the mixture into each thigh and each drumstick.

Next, season the turkey very liberally with Creole seasoning and black pepper. Tuck the wings behind the bird. Set aside at room temperature for at least 1 hour or in the refrigerator for up to 24 hours before cooking.

Frying Your Turkey

Before you begin frying, be sure your outdoor fryer is set up in a safe location away from anything flammable. Then clip a deep-frying thermometer securely to the side of the pot, fill the pot with peanut oil to the marked line, remove the tape, and begin heating the oil.

When the oil reaches 350°F, following the instructions of your fryer and rig, gently lower the turkey into the oil. The oil temperature will drop right away, but keep an eye on it, controlling it so that it goes back up to 350°F and then maintaining that temperature.

Fry the turkey until it is golden brown and fully cooked through, 30 to 45 minutes. To test for doneness, lift the turkey from the oil and insert an instant-read thermometer into the thickest part of the thigh and the breast. It should read 165°F in the thigh and 150°F in the breast. Once the turkey is cooked, let it rest for 10 minutes before carving.

Carving Your Turkey

Using a sharp knife, separate the leg quarters from the breast and then cut down between the drumsticks and thighs (the drumstick is a trophy and ready to serve), separating them into individual pieces. Separate the thigh meat from the bone and then cut it into slices, discarding the bone. Next, slice the turkey breast from the side, cutting into thin serving slices. Alternately, you can remove the breast halves from the breast bones and slice them crosswise.

Leftover turkey will keep, tightly covered, in the refrigerator for up to 6 days.

Smoked Prime Rib

I love prime rib, both smoked and roasted. When I'm smoking a turkey, I like putting a prime rib in with it. During the holidays, I love the smell of hickory at six o'clock on a cold, brisk morning with a cup of coffee and some jazz going.

Prime rib is a big hunk of meat and can seem intimidating, but is so easy. I like it cooked medium, but do yours however you like. It's one of my favorite holiday things. There are a lot of traditions in my family, but I started this one, dammit.

Prime rib should be seasoned for at least an hour in advance of smoking, or for up to a whole day ahead if you can.

1 prime rib roast (about 9 pounds)

Salted butter, at room temperature, for rubbing

Coarsely ground black pepper

About 1½ cups Bludso's Steak Rub (page 48)

3 tablespoons dried rosemary leaves (optional)

2 cups beef broth

JUS

Beef drippings from the drip pan

1 cup beef broth

1 tablespoon finely chopped garlic

Kosher salt

Wood: Hickory and pecan

Temperature: 240° to 250°F

Rough Cook Time: 4 or 6 hours (This really depends on the size of the prime rib.)

Cooking Equipment: Smoker, drip pan, mop or brush, instant-read thermometer, medium saucepan

Seasoning Your Prime Rib

Dry off your prime rib with a paper or kitchen towel. Rub a thin, even layer of butter all over the prime rib, then liberally season with pepper, followed by the steak rub and then the dried rosemary (if using). Gently rub in the seasonings. Allow the prime rib to marinate at room temperature for at least 1 hour or in the refrigerator for up to 24 hours.

Smoking Your Prime Rib

Follow the instructions in How to Light Your Pit (page 39), aiming for a temperature of 250°F. When the charcoal is ready, start with about 70 percent hickory and 30 percent pecan. Let the wood burn off for 5 to 10 minutes.

When the pit is ready, place a drip pan under the rack, then place the prime rib, fat-side up, on the rack above the pan. Now keep an eye on the temperature. Every time the temperature drops to 240°F, add a little more wood and charcoal.

After 2 hours, open the pit and mop your prime rib with the beef broth. Check the internal temperature of the roast with an instant-read thermometer to see if it is cooked to your liking. On a smaller roast, it could be just about done, but a larger one could still have 2 hours to go. Continue smoking, mopping with broth every time you open the pit, until your prime rib is ready. I like mine cooked to medium, so I pull it off at 135°F (the temperature will rise 5 to 10 degrees while the roast is resting). Mop the prime rib one last time just before it comes out of the pit, then let rest for 20 minutes before carving.

To make the jus: While the roast is resting, pour the drippings from the drip pan into a medium saucepan. Add the beef broth and garlic, place over medium-high heat, and bring to a boil. Turn the heat to a simmer and let simmer for 5 minutes. Season with salt, then remove from the heat and keep warm.

Carving Your Prime Rib

You can slice a prime rib any way you want. Some people even just cut right in between the bones and serve them like huge steaks. But if I want to serve slices, I like to just carve it right there on the bone and then separate the slices from the bone after.

Leftover prime rib will keep, tightly covered, in the refrigerator for up to 6 days.

Candied Yams

Here's one recipe that will get your sugar up quick. That smell of brown sugar early in the morning when my mom used to make these yams brings me back to childhood.

This is a holiday essential that's also a Sunday-dinner staple. It's nice and sweet, like a sweet potato pie but without all the work. I don't really have a sweet tooth, but I've got to have candied yams on my holiday plate, baby.

MAKES 6 TO 8 SERVINGS

4½ pounds medium-to-large yams

1 cup water

1½ cups granulated sugar

1½ cups packed dark brown sugar

1½ tablespoons ground cinnamon

1½ teaspoons ground nutmeg

1½ teaspoons vanilla extract

Kosher salt

¾ cup salted butter, roughly sliced and at room temperature

Cooking Equipment: Wide, medium pot or Dutch oven with a lid

Peel the yams, then cut them crosswise into ¼-inch-thick slices. They should look like medallions.

Fill a wide, medium pot or Dutch oven with enough water to cover the yams (once they are added) and bring to a boil over high heat. Add the yams, turn the heat to a gentle simmer, and cook, uncovered, just until slightly softened, about 15 minutes. Drain the yams and discard the water.

Add the 1 cup water and half of the yam slices to the pot and place over medium heat. Add 1 cup of the granulated sugar, 1 cup of the brown sugar, 1 tablespoon of the cinnamon, 1 teaspoon of the nutmeg, 1 teaspoon of the vanilla, and ¼ teaspoon salt. The sugars and seasonings can all rest right on top of the yams. Top with the remaining yam slices and then the remaining ½ cup granulated sugar, ½ cup brown sugar, ½ tablespoon cinnamon, ½ teaspoon nutmeg, ½ teaspoon vanilla, and another ¼ teaspoon salt.

Partially cover the pot with the lid and allow the yams to cook as the sugars melt. Keep an eye on the heat and adjust as needed so the liquid never goes above a gentle simmer. Stir occasionally and gently, making sure not to let the sugar burn and trying not to break up the yam slices. Continue simmering until the yams are tender, about 30 minutes.

Remove the pot from the heat, top with the butter, and then re-cover to allow the butter to melt. Keep covered for 5 minutes and then stir gently. Taste for seasoning and adjust with salt, if needed. The yams can sit for an hour or so before serving; if they have cooled too much, make sure to reheat them gently.

Leftover yams will keep in an airtight container in the refrigerator for up 6 days.

Cornbread Dressing

It's no Thanksgiving without dressing. But I don't need a holiday for some good dressing, either. It's more than a holiday staple. I want to give you a recipe that you can make in the middle of the year, because you never know when you're gonna want it on a Wednesday in March for no reason or for a Sunday dinner that doesn't have anything to do with a holiday.

I enhance my dressing with a lot of things, but you don't have to. Like so many recipes in this book, this one's all about layering flavors, and it all starts with your broth.

MAKES 6 TO 8 SERVINGS

Preheat the oven to 350°F. Thoroughly grease a 9 by 13-inch baking dish with vegetable shortening (I prefer butter-flavored Crisco).

In a large bowl, combine the cornbread and crackers and crumble by hand into uniform coarse crumbs. Add the eggs and stir until completely mixed, then add the sage and thyme and mix thoroughly. Now add the celery, onion, garlic, chicken, gizzards, and broth and stir until the ingredients are evenly distributed and the mixture is uniformly moistened. Add more broth if needed to achieve a moist but not overly wet consistency, mixing again until completely incorporated. Transfer the mixture to the prepared baking dish, spreading it in an even layer.

Bake the dressing until the center is hot and the top is golden brown, about 45 minutes. To check for doneness, insert a small knife blade into the center for a few seconds, then remove it and touch the blade; it should feel hot. Cover to keep warm until serving.

Leftover dressing will keep, tightly covered, in the refrigerator for up to 6 days.

1½ recipes Cornbread (page 199)

15 Ritz crackers

2 eggs, lightly beaten

1 teaspoon ground sage

1 teaspoon ground thyme

1 cup finely chopped celery

¼ cup finely chopped yellow onion

1 teaspoon finely chopped garlic

2 cups pulled cooked chicken thigh meat (from Thanksgiving Broth, page 239)

1 cup finely chopped cooked gizzards (from Thanksgiving Broth, page 239)

4 cups Thanksgiving Broth (page 239), or as needed

Cooking Equipment: 9 by 13-inch baking dish

Giblet Gravy

I cannot have my dressing without giblet gravy. I like eggs in my gravy, and I've asked everybody in my family why we put eggs in the gravy. They all just say, "I don't know. That's the way my momma did it." You don't have to do it. And I don't think it messes with the taste if you leave them out, but I love it.

Some people don't even like the gizzards, but I love them too. I used to steal some out of the pot when my mom was boiling them, and I think they're the perfect appetizer.

MAKES ABOUT 6 CUPS

3½ cups Thanksgiving Broth (facing page), or as needed

½ cup evaporated milk

½ cup all-purpose flour

½ cup finely chopped cooked gizzards (from Thanksgiving Broth, facing page)

½ cup finely chopped celery

¼ cup finely chopped yellow onion

1 teaspoon finely chopped garlic

3 hard-boiled eggs, peeled and finely chopped

Ground black pepper

Kosher salt

Cooking Equipment: Large skillet or sauté pan

In a large skillet or sauté pan over medium heat, combine the broth, evaporated milk, and flour and whisk until thoroughly mixed and smooth. Then continue whisking just until the mixture begins to bubble and the raw flour taste is gone, about 4 minutes. Add the gizzards, celery, onion, garlic, eggs, and ½ teaspoon pepper and mix thoroughly.

Bring the mixture back just to a simmer, then turn the heat to low and let simmer for 5 minutes, stirring occasionally, until you have a medium gravy consistency. Taste for seasoning and adjust with salt and pepper, if needed. Set aside off the heat, covered, until it's time to serve. (If you need to rewarm the gravy, you can add a tiny bit more broth and reheat it very gently over low heat.)

Leftover gravy will keep in an airtight container in the refrigerator for up to 5 days.

Thanksgiving Broth

**Excellent Giblet Gravy (facing page) and Cornbread Dressing
(page 237) start with an excellent broth—and this is excellent broth. I
call for lots of gizzards here because I love snacking on them straight
out of the pot all day long. Add the gizzards last because they can
stick to the bottom of the pot.**

**This broth is used in the gravy and dressing recipes and so will the
cooked gizzards and pulled meat from the chicken thighs. (The necks
will have lost their flavor.) But this is also just a great broth to have
on hand that you can use for any other cooking that you want to do.**

MAKES ABOUT 3 QUARTS

In a large stockpot over high heat, combine the chicken thighs, turkey necks,
onion, garlic, bouillon powder, and gizzards. Add water to cover the meat
by about 2 inches, cover the pot, and bring to a boil. Then turn the heat to
a simmer and let simmer, covered, until the meat is tender and the broth is
flavorful, about 2 hours.

Strain the broth through a fine-mesh sieve and set aside the broth and gizzards
and chicken meat separately; discard the turkey necks (they will have lost their
flavor). Both the broth and the meats will be used for gravy and dressing, with
some left over for other uses.

The broth will keep in an airtight container in the refrigerator for up to 6 days,
or in the freezer for up to 4 months. It will have some fat in there so just make
sure you stir before using in other recipes. The meats will keep in an airtight
container in the refrigerator for up to 1 week.

5 pounds chicken thighs

2½ pounds turkey necks

1 cup finely chopped yellow onion

¼ cup finely chopped garlic

½ cup chicken bouillon powder

12 pounds chicken gizzards

Cooking Equipment: Large stockpot

SWEETEST THINGS I'VE EVER KNOWN

These are all the end-of-the-nighters. I'm not a huge dessert person, other than some Hennessy on the Rocks, and now that I'm getting older, I've gotta save my sugars for some cognac. But late at night, after you're buzzed and there's a piece of Mom's Blackberry Cobbler, you hit it in the microwave, then put it with some Blue Bell ice cream and sneak it back into your room? That's some good shit. I don't eat a lot of desserts, but do I love them.

Hennessy on the Rocks

This is my ETD—"End of The Day." First of all, it's got to be in a glass. Don't come at me with no cup. Second, three nice cubes of ice. They don't have to be the big ones. Third, double shot. This is my drink of choice. One thing my granny always said about cognac: find you a drink that's a little expensive, that way your broke ass can't become an alcoholic.

I smoke my meat low and slow, and I like my Hennessy a solid po', and give me some mo'.

MAKES 1 SERVING

1 to 3 ice cubes

Double shot of Hennessy

Put the ice into a rocks glass. Pour in the Hennessy. Sip and repeat.

Mom's Baked Banana Pudding

This is one of those things that I have to have whenever my mom makes it. Her baked banana pudding is so much better than the classic one out of the box. When I was young, the smell in the house when she was making this pudding was just incredible. She used to get out a spoon and let me taste it just when she pulled it off the stove, so now whenever I have it, it brings back memories.

MAKES 8 TO 10 SERVINGS

Preheat the oven to 350°F.

Separate the eggs, putting the yolks in a medium bowl and setting the whites aside. Lightly beat the yolks until blended.

In a 3-quart saucepan over medium-low heat, combine the evaporated milk, 2 cups of the sugar, the flour, and salt and cook, stirring constantly, until the mixture is bubbling around the edges and thickly coats the back of the spoon, 25 to 30 minutes. Whisk about ¼ cup or so of the evaporated milk mixture into the beaten egg yolks to temper them, then slowly pour the tempered eggs back into the saucepan while whisking constantly. Continue whisking until fully incorporated, 2 to 3 minutes. Remove the pan from the heat and stir in the butter and vanilla extract until the butter melts. Transfer the pudding to a heatproof bowl and cover with plastic wrap, pressing directly against the surface of the pudding to prevent a skin from forming.

Place a layer of vanilla wafers along the bottom and up the sides of 2½-quart ovenproof glass bowl or baking dish. Next, peel and slice the bananas and arrange one-third of the slices in a layer on top of the wafers on the bottom of the container. Then either spoon or pour one-third of the pudding on top of the bananas. Arrange half of the remaining vanilla wafers on top of the pudding layer, then top the pudding layer with half of the remaining banana slices, followed by half of the remaining pudding. Repeat the layers one more time with the remaining vanilla wafers, banana slices, and pudding. Set aside in the refrigerator.

In a stand mixer fitted with the whisk attachment, or in a large bowl using a handheld mixer, on medium speed, beat together the egg whites and cream of tartar until frothy. Increase the speed to medium-high and beat until soft peaks form. Then slowly add the remaining ¼ cup sugar, a little at a time, and beat until you have a very stiff meringue.

Spread the meringue on top of the pudding, taking care to cover it completely. The meringue can sit above the rim of the bowl. If you still have some banana slices, you can garnish the meringue with them.

Bake the pudding until the meringue is just golden brown, about 10 minutes. Remove from the oven and let cool for 15 minutes. Serve the pudding warm, or let cool completely, cover, refrigerate, and serve chilled.

Leftover pudding will keep, tightly covered, in the refrigerator for up to 5 days.

4 eggs

Two 12-ounce cans evaporated milk

2¼ cups granulated sugar

6 tablespoons all-purpose flour

½ teaspoon kosher salt

4 tablespoons chilled unsalted butter, cut into small pieces

1 tablespoon vanilla extract

One 14-ounce box vanilla wafers

5 or 6 large, ripe bananas

½ teaspoon cream of tartar

Cooking Equipment: 3-quart saucepan, 2½-quart ovenproof glass bowl or baking dish, stand mixer with whisk attachment or handheld mixer

Julie's Bourbon-Pecan Bread Pudding

While I've been living out in Texas, my neighbors Julie and Charles, who live right next door, became great friends and not just neighbors. Julie is from New Orleans and is an incredible cook. She's the first person who ever served me great sautéed greens. She's a down-home chef who makes incredible Louisiana cuisine, and her bread pudding with a cognac topping is so rich and so good. My granny made bread pudding, too, so you know Julie's has to be something special if I'm putting hers in my book instead of Granny's.

Julie also wants you to know, "Yeah, yeah–get over the fact that a water bath is the best way to cook bread pudding!"

Any stale white bread will work for this recipe, though something with a flaky crust and airy interior is best. Just don't use one that's especially dense or one with seeds, whole grains, or cornmeal.

MAKES 8 TO 10 SERVINGS

1 pound day-old white bread (such as French bread, pistolettes, or bolillos), toasted in the oven just until it crisps a bit

½ cup pecan pieces, toasted

½ cup dried currants or golden raisins, soaked in ¼ cup bourbon for about 15 minutes, drained, and bourbon reserved

5 eggs

6 cups whole milk

¾ cup granulated sugar

¾ cup packed dark brown sugar

2 tablespoons vanilla extract or bourbon

½ teaspoon ground cinnamon

⅛ teaspoon ground nutmeg

Preheat the oven to 350°F. Butter a 9 by 13-inch baking dish.

Tear the bread into about-2-inch chunks and add to the prepared baking dish. Sprinkle with the pecans and currants, toss to combine, and then spread the mixture in an even layer.

In a large bowl, whisk the eggs until foamy. Add the milk, both sugars, vanilla, cinnamon, and nutmeg and whisk to combine. Pour the egg mixture evenly over the bread mixture, adding just enough to cover the bread pieces (you may have some mixture left). Let the bread soak for 5 minutes, occasionally gently pressing down on it with the back of a spoon. The bread should be quite saturated; if it looks a little dry, add more of the egg mixture and then discard the rest.

Meanwhile, in a kettle or a saucepan, bring about 6 cups water to a boil. Place the baking dish inside a larger, deep baking pan and transfer the baking pan to the oven. Add enough of the boiling water to the baking pan to come halfway up the sides of the baking dish.

Bake the pudding until set and no liquid remains on the surface, about 1 hour. The edges of the bread should be light brown without too much darkening or any burning. If the pudding is not quite set but the top is nicely browned, cover loosely with aluminum foil and continue to bake until a knife inserted into the center comes out clean. When the pudding is ready, remove from the oven and let rest in the water bath for 10 minutes, then carefully remove the pudding dish from the water bath.

CONTINUED

Julie's Bourbon-Pecan Bread Pudding, continued

To make the sauce: While the pudding rests, in a medium saucepan over medium heat, combine the butter and both sugars. Warm, stirring occasionally, until the butter has melted, the sugars have dissolved, and the mixture is just bubbling. Add the bourbon and salt and continue to cook, stirring constantly, for about 5 minutes to cook off the alcohol. Remove from the heat and whisk in the cream until fully combined.

Serve the pudding warm, with the bourbon sauce spooned over the top.

Leftover bread pudding and sauce will keep separately, tightly covered, in the refrigerator for up to 5 days.

BOURBON SAUCE

1½ cups unsalted butter

1 cup packed dark brown sugar

½ cup granulated sugar

¾ cup bourbon, plus bourbon reserved from soaking currants

1 pinch kosher salt

½ cup heavy cream

Cooking Equipment: 9 by 13-inch baking dish; large, deep baking pan; medium saucepan

Shirley Ann's Buttermilk Pie

Granny used to make buttermilk pie; when I was younger, I was able to eat a whole pie by myself. This is another one of my favorite desserts that you hardly ever see in LA; but in Texas, you can get it at the damn gas station.

The closest person who can still do this pie just like my granny is my cousin Shirley Ann. So now it's something I can still get from her if I want one.

MAKES 8 SERVINGS

9-inch deep-dish piecrust shell

½ cup unsalted butter,
at room temperature

1¼ cups granulated sugar

3 tablespoons all-purpose flour

¼ teaspoon fine sea salt

3 eggs

1 cup buttermilk

1 tablespoon fresh lemon juice

1 teaspoon vanilla extract

⅛ teaspoon ground nutmeg

Cooking Equipment: Stand mixer with whisk attachment or handheld mixer, baking sheet

Preheat the oven to 350°F. Have the piecrust ready in its pie pan.

In a stand mixer fitted with the whisk attachment, or in a large bowl and using a handheld mixer, on medium speed, beat together the butter and sugar, slowly increasing the speed to medium-high, until creamy and smooth, 2 to 3 minutes. Add the flour, salt, and eggs and continue to beat on medium-high speed until smooth, 2 to 3 minutes. Then add the buttermilk, lemon juice, vanilla, and nutmeg and beat until well mixed. The mixture may look curdled, but that is okay. Pour the mixture into the piecrust. Set the pie pan on a baking sheet and transfer to the oven.

Bake the pie until it is golden brown on top and the center just barely jiggles (but is not liquid) when the pie pan is gently shaken, 50 to 55 minutes. (The filling will continue to set as it cools.) Transfer the pie to a wire rack and let cool completely before slicing and serving.

Leftover pie will keep, tightly covered, in the refrigerator for up to 6 days.

Mom's Blackberry Cobbler

This was a Sunday dessert. When I got old enough to be out on my own, playing ball or at a friend's house to watch the game, I'd always come home if Mom was cooking Sunday dinner. If you were lucky, she was also making this blackberry cobbler, which she served fresh out of the oven and with a couple scoops of homemade vanilla ice cream. Even as a kid, I suffered from those Monday-morning blues, so she used this to make me happy and get me home.

Some people might say that they've never heard of a cobbler that has a bottom crust. But I've never heard of a cobbler that *didn't* have a bottom crust. If you choose not to go the lattice route, my mom says you can make the top of your cobbler however you want and it will still taste great, but a lattice does look the best. This kind of food will bring memories to your family just like it does for me. I'm blessed to have my mom here still. If I ask her to make it, she'll talk a gang of shit but she'll still make it.

Preheat the oven to 350°F.

To make the crust dough: In a large bowl, stir together the flour, granulated sugar, and salt, mixing well. Add the shortening and, using a pastry blender or a fork, work it into the flour mixture until crumbly and the bits of shortening are the size of peas.

In a medium bowl, whisk together the eggs, water, and vinegar. Add most of the liquid to the flour mixture and stir together with a fork until all the ingredients are evenly moistened and the dough holds together, adding more water if needed. If the mixture is too wet, you can add a little more flour. The dough should hold its shape and be neither tacky nor crumbly and dry. Knead the dough in the bowl to bring it together into a smooth ball.

Lightly flour a large work surface and turn the dough onto it. Divide the dough in half and set half aside, covering it with plastic wrap. Using a floured rolling pin, roll out the other half into a rectangle about 14 by 18 inches and ⅛ to ¼ inch thick. Roll the dough up on the rolling pin, then unfurl it over a 9 by 13-inch baking dish, easing it onto the bottom and up the sides. Trim any excess, leaving a 1-inch overhang. If the dough tears, don't worry about it; just press it back together in the dish.

Flour the work surface again. Take the remaining dough ball, cut it in half, and roll one half into a rectangle about 6 by 15 inches and ⅛ to ¼ inch thick. Cover with a kitchen towel and set aside. Flour the surface again, take the final dough ball, and roll it into a rectangle about 6 by 11 inches and ⅛ to ¼ inch thick. Cover with another kitchen towel and set aside. (For easier handling, transfer the doughs to floured parchment and store them, covered, in the refrigerator, until it is time to cut them and weave the lattice.)

CONTINUED

MAKES 8 TO 10 SERVINGS

COBBLER CRUST

8 cups all-purpose flour, or as needed

2 tablespoons granulated sugar

4 teaspoons kosher salt

2½ cups chilled vegetable shortening

2 eggs

1 cup water, or as needed

2 tablespoons distilled white vinegar

COBBLER FILLING

3 cups canned or frozen blackberries

1 cup packed light brown sugar

2 teaspoons fresh lemon juice

2 tablespoons cornstarch

1 teaspoon ground cinnamon

1 teaspoon vanilla extract

1 pinch kosher salt

Cooking Equipment: Rolling pin, 9 by 13-inch baking dish, large baking sheet

Mom's Blackberry Cobbler, continued

To make the filling: In a medium bowl, combine the blackberries, brown sugar, lemon juice, cornstarch, cinnamon, vanilla, and salt. Stir to mix well.

Pour the filling into the prepared baking dish. Using a chef's knife, cut each reserved sheet of dough, long-ways, into even 1-inch-wide strips. Evenly place the six longest strips across the length of the filling. Evenly weave in the six shorter strips across the width of the filling to form a lattice top. Crimp together the ends of the strips with the bottom crust overhang, trimming off any excess dough. Place the baking dish on a large baking sheet and transfer to the oven.

Bake the cobbler until the filling has thick bubbling in the center and the pastry is light golden brown, about 1 hour. Let the cobbler rest for about 10 minutes before serving.

Leftover cobbler will keep, tightly covered, in the refrigerator for up to 6 days.

Thelma's Cheesecake

My old classmate Thelma and her husband, Rico, were coming to visit me down in Corsicana every weekend for a while. I always give Thelma shit for her cooking and her personality, but I kept her coming around because she cleans the hell out of the kitchen for me before they leave every Sunday. One night, after a few cocktails, I felt so damn guilty about all the cleaning that I promised her she could put a recipe in my damn book.

The truth is, Thelma is a great cook. And with all the cooking we were doing during the pandemic, she and Rico were the only people I allowed to be down here with me, which shows I have a lot of trust in them. So here is her recipe for a damn good cheesecake. It needs to chill for at least 4 hours before serving, so plan accordingly. The filling can be made in a stand mixer fitted with the paddle attachment, a medium bowl using a handheld mixer, or a medium bowl with a wooden spoon.

MAKES 6 TO 8 SERVINGS

CHEESECAKE CRUST

One 4½-ounce sleeve graham crackers (about 9 crackers)

3 tablespoons salted butter, melted

2½ tablespoons granulated sugar

CHEESECAKE FILLING

19 ounces cream cheese, at room temperature

1 cup granulated sugar

3 eggs

1 tablespoon vanilla extract

1 teaspoon lemon extract

1 teaspoon grated lemon zest

Fresh fruit or fruit pie filling of your choice for topping (optional)

Cooking Equipment: 8-inch round springform pan, stand mixer with paddle attachment or handheld mixer (optional)

To make the crust: Preheat the oven to 300°F.

Put the graham crackers into a plastic bag and crush completely. (You can use a rolling pin or the bottom of a heavy skillet.) Transfer the crumbs to a medium bowl, add the butter and sugar, and toss until the crumbs are evenly moistened.

Lightly coat the bottom and sides of an 8-inch round springform pan with nonstick cooking spray. Pour the crumb mixture into the pan, then press it onto bottom and up the sides as firmly as possible (a rubber spatula helps).

Bake the crust until set and fragrant, about 5 minutes. Let cool on a wire rack.

To make the filling: In a bowl, combine the cream cheese and sugar and beat until smooth and creamy. Add the eggs, one at a time, beating after each addition until the mixture is smooth. Add the vanilla, lemon extract, and lemon zest and beat until thoroughly mixed.

Add the filling to the crust, return the pan to the oven, and bake until the surface of the cheesecake is firm to the touch, 1 hour to 1 hour and 10 minutes. Transfer to a wire rack and let cool completely, then chill for 4 hours.

When ready to serve, unclasp and lift off the pan sides. You can leave the cheesecake on the pan bottom or, using a wide offset spatula, carefully transfer it to a cake plate. If using fruit or fruit pie filling, spread it over the top of the cheesecake.

Leftover cheesecake will keep, tightly covered, in the refrigerator for up to 6 days.

Nancy's Red Velvet Cake

When we were opening up Bludso's Hollywood, Noah was running the kitchen, and he had his mom, Nancy, making all the pies and the red velvet cake. Noah was so damn tired and stressed out back then. But one thing I always emphasize about Bludso's is that we are a family. So when I first met Nancy, we were sitting down together at the restaurant breaking bread and sampling some of her pies.

Nancy was a sweetheart, but she was so concerned about her son. Then we got to talking and she realized, "Kevin is his big brother and he's got him. He's got my son." As crazy as Noah can be, she knew I could handle his ass and would look out for him. Then I felt the comfort in her knowing that I had his back, and we both felt that love. She was looking after her baby. That was a mama bear making sure nobody was fucking with her son.

But then on top of that, Nancy is an incredible baker and has made some of the best desserts I've ever tasted, and her shit is real. Not everybody's mama can cook, but Nancy really can.

MAKES 8 SERVINGS

2½ cups cake flour (not self-rising)

¼ cup unsweetened natural cocoa powder

1 teaspoon kosher salt

1½ cups granulated sugar

1½ cups canola oil

2 eggs

¼ cup liquid red food coloring

1 teaspoon vanilla extract

1 cup buttermilk

1½ teaspoons baking soda

2 teaspoons distilled white vinegar

CREAM CHEESE FROSTING

½ cup unsalted butter, at room temperature

8 ounces cream cheese, at room temperature

1 cup confectioners' sugar

1 teaspoon vanilla extract

Cooking Equipment: Two 9 by 2-inch round cake pans, stand mixer with paddle attachment

Preheat the oven to 350°F. Generously butter and flour the bottom and sides of two 9 by 2-inch round cake pans. Tap out the excess and set aside.

In a medium bowl, whisk together the flour, cocoa powder, and salt. Set aside.

In a stand mixer fitted with the paddle attachment, combine the granulated sugar and canola oil and beat on medium speed until well mixed. Add the eggs, one at a time, beating after each addition until fully incorporated. Add the food coloring and continue beating until evenly mixed.

With the mixer still on medium speed, add the flour mixture, ½ cup at a time, alternating with the buttermilk, about ¼ cup at a time, until all of the flour mixture and the buttermilk have been fully incorporated. Stop to scrape down the sides of the bowl with a spatula as needed.

In a small bowl, stir together the baking soda and vinegar, then add to the batter and beat on medium speed for another 10 seconds. Evenly divide the batter among the prepared pans. Tap each pan on a countertop a few times to release any air bubbles.

Bake the cakes until a cake tester or toothpick inserted into the center of each comes out clean, 30 to 35 minutes. Transfer to wire racks to let cool in the pans for about 5 minutes. Run a small knife blade around the inside edge of a pan to loosen the cake sides, then invert the cake onto the rack, lift off the pan, and turn the cake layer right-side up to cool completely. Repeat with the second cake.

To make the frosting: While the cake layers are cooling, rinse and dry the mixer bowl and paddle and return them to the mixer stand.

Add the butter to the bowl and beat on medium speed until light and fluffy, 2 to 3 minutes. Add the cream cheese and beat until light and fluffy, 2 to 3 minutes more. Add the confectioners' sugar and vanilla and continue to beat until the sugar is fully incorporated and the frosting is smooth, about 2 minutes more. Cover and set aside.

When the cake layers have completely cooled, using a serrated knife (like a bread knife) and a sawing motion, slice off the domed top from each layer, creating a flat top. Place one layer on a cake plate. Using an offset spatula, spread a ½-inch-thick layer of the frosting across the top of the cake. Place the second cake layer on top, sandwiching the frosting between the rounds.

Spread a thin layer of the frosting around the sides and over the top of the cake. This is known as a crumb coat, and it will prevent any visible crumbs in the final coat of frosting. Place the cake in the refrigerator for 20 minutes to set the crumb coat. Now, frost the sides and the top of the cake with the remaining frosting.

Cut the cake into wedges and serve.

Leftover cake will keep, tightly covered, in the refrigerator for up to 5 days.

Mom's Strawberry Cake

This cake takes me back to being a little, little kid. Mom used to feed me this when I was so young. I love eating it with an ice-cold glass of milk. I take a bite of this and it brings me right to my childhood. This might be, out of all of Mom's desserts, her best one. I always wanted it for my birthday.

MAKES 6 TO 8 SERVINGS

Preheat the oven to 350°F. Line the bottoms of three 9 by 3-inch round cake pans with parchment or wax paper and lightly coat the paper and the sides of the pans with nonstick cooking spray.

In the bowl of a stand mixer fitted with the whisk attachment, or in a large bowl and using a handheld mixer, on medium speed, beat together the cake mix, flour, vegetable oil, and water until thoroughly combined, 1 to 2 minutes. Add the eggs, one at a time, beating after each addition until fully incorporated, 2 to 3 minutes. Add the gelatin powder and beat until incorporated. Using a rubber spatula, fold in the strawberries. Evenly divide the batter among the prepared pans. Tap each pan on a countertop a few times to release any air bubbles.

Bake the cakes until a cake tester or toothpick inserted into the center of each comes out clean, about 25 minutes. Transfer to wire racks to let cool completely. Run a small knife blade around the inside edge of a pan to loosen the cake sides, then invert the cake onto the rack, lift off the pan, peel off the paper, and turn the cake layer right-side up. Repeat with the remaining two cake layers.

To make the frosting: While the cake layers are cooling, rinse and dry the mixer bowl and whisk attachment, if using a stand mixer, or the bowl and beaters, if using a handheld mixer.

Spread the strawberries in a sieve set over a bowl to drain off as much liquid as possible (otherwise you will have a wet frosting).

In the bowl, combine the butter, cream cheese, confectioners' sugar, and well-drained berries and beat on medium-high speed until light and fluffy. If the frosting is a little thin, beat in a little more confectioners' sugar. Transfer the frosting to the refrigerator to chill and allow to stiffen until ready to frost the cake.

Place one cake layer on a plate or platter. Using an offset spatula, spread the top with a thin layer of the frosting, then top with a second cake layer and spread it with a thin layer of frosting. (If you like, you can place some strawberry slices on the frosting on each layer.) As you are frosting the first two layers, make sure to reserve enough frosting to cover the entire outside of the cake. Place the third cake layer on top, then spread the remaining frosting on the sides and the top of the cake. Decorate the top with strawberry slices.

Cut the cake into wedges and serve.

Leftover cake will keep, tightly covered, in the refrigerator for up to 5 days.

One 21-ounce package, or one and a half 15.25-ounce packages, white cake mix

¼ cup all-purpose flour

1 cup vegetable oil

½ cup water

4 eggs

One 3-ounce package strawberry gelatin powder

1 cup finely chopped fresh strawberries

STRAWBERRY FROSTING

¾ cup finely chopped fresh strawberries

½ cup unsalted butter, at room temperature

8 ounces cream cheese, at room temperature

1 pound confectioners' sugar, or as needed

Sliced strawberries for decorating

Cooking Equipment: Three 9 by 3-inch round cake pans, parchment or wax paper, stand mixer with whisk attachment or handheld mixer

How I Like to Chill

I just want to send a quick shout-out to a few of my favorite establishments (and people). Some are still here and some are long gone, but these are the places that I cherished as a kid growing up, and during my life and my travels as an adult. If you're ever in any of these areas, check some out because they're very special to my heart.

Ackee Bamboo
4305 Degnan Blvd., Los Angeles, CA 90008

Aggie General
8803 US-287, Corsicana, TX 75109

Aunty Martha's Kitchen (closed)

Bates Fish Market
2206 W. El Segundo Blvd., Gardena, CA 90249

Chico's Pizza Parlor
12120 Long Beach Blvd., Lynwood, CA 90262

Cofax Coffee
440 N. Fairfax Ave., Los Angeles, CA 90036

C W & Chris Fish and Chicken
6512 S. Western Ave., Los Angeles, CA 90047

The Dairy
701 S. Long Beach Blvd., Compton, CA 90221

Darrow's New Orleans Grill
21720 S. Avalon Blvd. #102, Carson, CA 90745

Dulan's
202 E. Manchester Blvd., Inglewood, CA 90301

Earle's On Crenshaw
3864 Crenshaw Blvd., Los Angeles, CA 90008

El Cholo—The Original
1121 S. Western Ave., Los Angeles, CA 90006

El Ranchito Restaurant
3401 S. Main St., Los Angeles, CA 90007

French Quarter Creole Bar & Grill
16728 Bellflower Blvd., Bellflower, CA 90706

Gadberry's Barbecue
5833 S. Broadway, Los Angeles, CA

Golden Bird Chicken
13501 S. Avalon Blvd., Los Angeles, CA 90061

Hambones BBQ & Po Boys
9342 Alondra Blvd., Bellflower, CA 90706

The Harbor Restaurant
10000 TX-294 Spur, Corsicana, TX 75109

Harold & Belle's
2920 W. Jefferson Blvd., Los Angeles, CA 90018

Hawkins House of Burgers
11603 Slater St., Los Angeles, CA 90059

Honey's Kettle Fried Chicken
9537 Culver Blvd., Culver City, CA 90232

Hotville Chicken
4070 Marlton Ave., Los Angeles, CA 90008

Jack Rabbit Liquor
1404 E. Alondra Blvd., Compton, CA 90221

Jack's Family Kitchen
3965 S. Western Ave, Los Angeles, CA 90062

Jay Bee's Bar-B-Q
15911 S. Avalon Blvd., Gardena, CA 90248

Jerry's Liquor
4279 S. Vermont Ave., Los Angeles, CA 90037

Jim Dandy Fried Chicken
11328 Vermont Ave., Los Angeles, CA 90044

Jinda Thai Restaurant
1/7 Ferguson St., Abbotsford VIC 3067, Australia

Jitlada
5233 Sunset Blvd., Los Angeles, CA 90027

Jordan's Hot Dogs
5960 Crenshaw Blvd., Los Angeles, CA 90043

King Taco
4504 E. 3rd St., Los Angeles, CA 90222

K&K Bar-b-que
1801 Martin Luther King Jr Blvd., Corsicana, TX 75110

Little Kingston Jamaican Restaurant
4716 W. Slauson Ave., Los Angeles, CA 90056

Louis Burgers II
1501 Rosecrans Ave., Compton, CA 90221

Manuel Dominguez High School Snack Bar
15301 S. San Jose Ave., Compton, CA 90221

Marathon Burger
621 E. Compton Blvd., Compton, CA 90221

Mom's Burgers
336 W. Alondra Blvd., Compton, CA 90220

Mr. Jim's (closed)

My Father's Barbeque
637 E. University Dr., Carson, CA 90746

Night + Market
9043 Sunset Blvd., West Hollywood, CA 90069

Oak Cove Café
10411 US-287, Corsicana, TX 75109

Phillips Bar-B-Que
2619 Crenshaw Blvd., Los Angeles, CA 90016

Prime Pizza
446 N. Fairfax Ave., Los Angeles, CA 90036

The Proud Bird
11022 Aviation Blvd., Los Angeles, CA 90045

Ramona's Mexican Food
728 Crenshaw Blvd., Los Angeles, CA 90016

R & R Soul Food
18427 S. Avalon Blvd., Carson, CA 90746

Rib Nest
1766 W. El Segundo Blvd., Gardena, CA 90249

RibsinLA
Weekly pop-up (www.ribsinla.com)

R Kitchen Soul Food
5253 Paramount Blvd., Lakewood, CA 90712

Robert Earl's BBQ
703 Artesia Blvd., Long Beach, CA 90805

Roosevelt Junior High Cafeteria
1200 E. Alondra Blvd., Compton, CA 90221

Roscoe's Chicken & Waffles
1514 N. Gower St., Los Angeles, CA 90028

Sally B's Liquor (closed)

Sal's Gumbo Shack
6148 Long Beach Blvd. W., Long Beach, CA 90805

San Pedro Fish Market & Restaurant
1190 Nagoya Way, San Pedro, CA 90731

Savoy Entertainment Center
218 S. La Brea Ave., Inglewood, CA 90301

The Serving Spoon
1403 Centinela Ave., Inglewood, CA 90302

Smhokin Pot
17944 S. Avalon Blvd., Carson, CA 90746

Smokin' Guns BBQ
2278 W. 7th Ave., Corsicana, TX 75110

Stevens Steak & Seafood House
5332 Stevens Pl., Commerce, CA 90040

T & C's Tackle Box Southern Seafood & More
17620 Bellflower Blvd., Bellflower, CA 90706

Taylor's Steak House
3361 W. 8th St., Los Angeles, CA 90005

Tortilleria Matehuala y Restaurante
105 W. 7th Ave., Corsicana, TX 75110

Tucker Town
4095 US-287, Corsicana, TX 75109

Veterans of Foreign Wars
303 E. Palmer St., Compton, CA 90221

Virgie's BBQ & Catering
5535 Gessner Dr., Houston, TX 77041

Watts Coffee House
1827 E. 103rd St., Los Angeles, CA 90002

Woody's Bar-B-Que
475 S. Market St., Inglewood, CA 90301

Paying Homage to Legendary (or Soon-to-Be Legendary) Pitmasters

JAMES BOATRIGHT

CAREY BRINGLE

SUSIE BULLOCH

TINA CANNON

MOE CASON

GEORGIA CHASEN

MICHAEL COLLINS

DR. HOWARD CONYERS

MELISSA COOKSTON

SYLVIE CURRY

CORY AND TARRA DAVIS

MADISON EAGLE

TYLER EAGLE

BRYAN FURMAN

OLLIE GATES

GREG GATLIN

GERRI GRADY

JAMES GRUBBS

PHIL JOHNSON

RASHAD JONES

SHALAMAR LANE

FRED LOC

AMY MILLS

ED MITCHELL

MYRON MIXON

HENRY PERRY

RASHEED PHILIPS

RODNEY SCOTT

RONALD SIMMONS

NEIL STRAWDER

TUFFY STONE

ASHLEY THOMPSON

HELEN TURNER

JIMMY WEATHERSBEE

LEE ANN WHIPPEN

A Note from the Coauthor

As a white guy from Santa Monica, California, the closest thing that I ever had to BBQ while growing up was a piece of grilled chicken with bottled BBQ sauce on it. So in 2011, when I tried Bludso's BBQ in Compton for the first time, it completely changed the way I thought about food. It rewired my brain. At the time, I was writing for *LA Weekly* and waiting tables at my friend James Starr's now-closed burger-and-beer café. During slow periods, James and I would stand around talking about ideas for restaurants to open. But we would always just end up saying, "How cool it would be if there was somewhere in LA where you could have a cocktail, eat Bludso's BBQ, and watch a game?"

It felt like a pipe dream but, over time, I got to talking to Kevin and wound up interviewing him for *LA Weekly.* Like always, Kevin gave an incredible interview. I played the tape for James when I got back that night, and he said, "Holy shit, we have to try to work with this guy." After a little back and forth about going into business, Kevin invited us to his granny's ninetieth birthday party in Corsicana, Texas. Kevin was kidding, I think, but James bought plane tickets. We showed up at the Martin Luther King Community Center in Corsicana, and when we arrived, everyone rightfully wondered what the hell we were doing there. Then Kevin came out and said in a booming voice, "These guys are really important to me, alright?" Everyone said, "Alright." By one o'clock in the morning, we were drinking corn rye, I'm pretty sure I was singing Sam Cooke songs with Kevin's auntie, and Kevin had agreed to go into business with us. About four hours later, we called him to see if he wanted to drive out to Lexington, Texas, to try Snow's BBQ, and, if I remember correctly, he said, "Y'all some real OGs. Let me know how it is." He didn't think we were going to get up.

Once we got back to LA, I was ready to start training in Compton. I showed up at four o'clock in the morning, and Kevin hadn't told anybody who I was or what I was doing there, so they just told me to go in the back and start cleaning collard greens and peeling potatoes. I remember thinking at the time, "Holy shit, I can't believe I get to work in the kitchen at Bludso's."

I trained in Compton for several months until we finally found our restaurant space for Bludso's Hollywood. We still hadn't hired anyone to run the kitchen, and for reasons I still don't entirely understand, Kevin and James told me that I should do it. I think I said no three times before I finally agreed. I remember telling Kevin, "I'm looking forward to those one-hundred-hour weeks," and he said, "One hundred hours!? Are you working part-time?" I thought he was kidding. He was not.

Opening that restaurant was when Kevin really became my big brother. The restaurant was a massive hit from Day One; and true to Kevin's word, I was working about one hundred FORTY hours a week. I made more than my fair share of stupid mistakes along the way, but Kevin knew how much I cared about looking after a restaurant with his name on it. Eventually, I got pretty burned out and wrecked by anxiety. I was seriously considering moving to Portland and becoming a bartender. That's when Kevin pulled me aside and told me not to make an emotional decision that I would regret. He told me that we were family and he had my back. He helped me take a breath and told me not to take everything so damn seriously all the time (he still tells me that).

We've been working together ever since, eating in restaurants around the country and even opening a BBQ restaurant inside of a casino in Melbourne, Australia. But, my favorite time over these last ten years of having Kevin as a friend and mentor was writing this book with him down in Corsicana. Over three separate trips, we would get up early, take turns doing treadmill workouts, drink healthful green smoothies, cook and write all day, and then sip cognac and rye and shoot the shit and listen to music at night. The next day, we would get up early and do it all over again. Looking back, it feels as something of a professional and personal culmination — and for the record, I should point out that there are few better things in the world than cooking food, having a few drinks, and talking shit with Kevin Bludso.

— Noah Galuten

Notes from the Photographers

My job on this book was simple: Do everything in my power to channel Big Kev and the memory of his granny. For every single photograph, I didn't stop working until I heard Kev say the words "Yeah, that feels right." Sometimes I nailed it right away. Other times—like the potato salad—things took a bit longer.

I started this project excited to hone my technique in Texas-style barbeque, but that turned out to be only a part of the story. In this book, Big Kev blows open the doors to his kitchen and shares personal family recipes that mean the world to him. I had come for the barbeque, but I fell in love with the soul food. This book is a treasure trove of both.

If anyone invites me over for Sunday dinner, I got the potato salad.

— Eric Wolfinger

Kev, wow, you did it. I never would have thought in a million years that you, hell, *we*, would be in the final phases of your first cookbook—me as one of your photographers, and you as the chef. I'm proud of you, homeboy; all the homies are proud of you. When you asked me if I wanted to be a photographer in your cookbook, all I could think of was, "We've come a long way." Back in the day, if you had asked me to shoot something, it would not have been a camera.

I sat back and thought of all the things that we've seen and experienced first-hand, and I realize being here today is nothing short of a miracle; someone did a lot of praying over us growing up. I want to thank you, Kev, for this opportunity to be a part of something positive while representing the city of Compton.

I'm sure that the readers who do not know me would never believe my story, and for those of you that do, know I will never change. From the East Side of Compton to the Marines and back, my word has always been solid. Kev, keep up the great work, you are making a lot of people proud.

— Demetrius Smith

Acknowledgments

Mommy, thank you for giving me my wings so that I may try to learn how to fly, even though you sometimes have to catch me when I fall! You are now, and always had to be, a little rough around the edges, raising three kids in Watts and Compton, but you did what you had to do to keep us safe and secure. Sometimes I don't know how you did it, but you always got it done! You were the first and finest example of a lady and how a lady should be in any situation: good and bad! I truly believe we are what mothers make us, and I'm thankful to you for making me into who I am.

Daddy, you are a true example of what it means to be a good person. Because of you, I learned to treat everyone with kindness and compassion. You taught me how to hunt, fish, play sports . . . and kick that ass when it was necessary! You taught me to always to be a gentleman and never let them see you sweat! You would always say, "I will never come visit you in prison," and that didn't hit home until some of my friends went to prison. Thank you for teaching me as a boy to always be a man.

Mrs. Ruth Tucker, my grandmother, thank you for kind of being a good sport when Granny would call me her grandson. (For those who don't know, my Granny is actually my great-auntie — my grandmother's sister.) Thank you for being you; for singing down-home blues at Iman's christening and for your special dance, "The Tuck." Thank you for showing me how to entertain people (your parties were legendary). I can't thank you enough for teaching my sisters, Debra, Sonia, Tanisha, Nikki, and Ashleigh, not to be ashamed to burp in public. I feel so sorry for their husbands. But most of all, thank you for my daddy.

James Starr, you saw something in me that even I didn't see. You earned the name "Big Game" by bringing this business where it is and through where it's going. My family knows your family and your family knows mine, so that's it. That means we are family. We had some tough decisions to make and some tough times to go through, but you had the confidence to get through them. I respect your calmness in a storm so much. But you also understand that this business is not just about us, it's about our families and their futures. This is just the beginning.

All my teachers and coaches, thank you. Shout out to the city of Compton, my hometown. The rough streets were also good streets. Thank you for all the tough love that you've shown me. My pastor, Rafer Owens, thank you for helping me become who I am; not just in the food world but really as a person. Thank you to all my teachers at Emerson Elementary, Roosevelt Junior High, and the mighty Dominguez High. Compton is a different place. Many people think they know Compton but truly they know nothing about it.

Corsicana, Texas, "The 'Can," how blessed am I to have two places to call home? Thank you for being the birthplace of my daddy. Thank you for the most memorable summers from the time I was nine years old;

the strawberry sodas, video games, fishing, chasing girls, staying up all night, catching lightening bugs, chasing trains, hanging out at Little Mama's, Kidd Jones, and the white bricks and the red bricks. Thank you for letting a city boy be a country boy even if it was just for the summer.

Monique, thank you for my beautiful kids. Thank you for your support and your incredible class. Thank you being the best co-pilot during this flight! You will always have a piece of my heart!

Aeryus, we never do steps around here! You are and always will be my son! And please understand that Paul is an incredible father and I thank him for sharing his fatherly duties and love with me! The man you've grown up to be is amazing but was no surprise to me. You have always swung for the fences! Soon to be Dr. Holloway; keep rising, A-bone!

Iman, my beautiful daughter, I've told you before and continue to tell you that the world is yours and waiting on you to claim it! You have a heart of gold and are beautiful inside and out! Queen Daughter, get the wind beneath your wings and soar to the heights where your many thrones await you! Always rise, Ma!

Dallas, the baby of my tribe, the one who sat back and observed everything that we all had to offer and then decided to become a sociologist. Hmmm, I wonder why . . . lol. I know why you have such a calming soul, and you naturally put people at ease! You're going to be my second doctor, and I couldn't be prouder. Keep rising, Dallas

My brothers and sisters, by being in the middle of eight beautiful siblings, I got to see both ends of the spectrum. We never did halves or steps in this family; we're all the same. We're all Bludsos. I loved you all as kids and I love you all as adults. This book has a little bit of each of us in it. David, rest in peace my big brother and my first bodyguard. Sonia, rest in peace. Deb, Tanisha, Nikki, Chris, and Ashley, thank you for the unconditional love and unconditional respect. Thank you to everyone for understanding their role in the hierarchy. I love you guys. I love your kids. Thank you for my nieces and nephews and doggies too.

Jon Taffer, thank you for taking me on the ride with you, for letting me play a small part in something so huge, for having the confidence in me, and for always calling me your good friend.

James Agiesta and Katy Dierks, thank you for being persistent. I know you hate hearing it but if it wasn't for you, I wouldn't be where I am in my television career. Thank you for staying on my niece until she made me go home and make that video for you all. Your tenacity got me my start.

GT and Jenn Taylor, thank you for making me feel so comfortable my first time on TV, like the cameras weren't even there. Every time I'm on TV, I judge the directors and producers off of you and who you were.

My Canadian family at *Fire Masters*, three years later we are still rocking. Thank you for allowing me to come to another country and do my thing, and for all the Canadian love. Mike Sharon and Jim Pratt and Lucky and Dylan and Rosie and all the judges and crew and everyone. Just know that if I didn't mention you, it's because my editor wouldn't let me put in any more names. I look forward to more long hours with good people, adding up to lasting memories.

The American Barbecue Showdown, Daniel Calin, Cat Sullivan, Dominic Ciccodicola, and all the rest of everybody – again, it is too many to name – who would have thought that on those hot days in Georgia, we were changing the way people think about and look at BBQ? I also want to thank my co-hosts, my fellow judges, and all the competitors.

Diners, Drive-Ins and Dives; *Bong Appétit*; *Man Fire Food*; *BBQ Brawl*; *Home & Family*; *Access Hollywood*; *TMZ*; *The Drew Barrymore Show*, KTLA, Fox, NBC, ABC – I want to give a shout-out to all of you.

All the media and writers that supported us early on, thank you. The *Los Angeles Times, LA Weekly, Corsicana Daily Sun, New York Times, Washington Post, USA Today,* LA Eater, Thrillist, The Infatuation, Jonathan Gold*,* Daniel Vaughn, Tony Chen, Robert from Yelp, and so many more.

My Compton staff, Cookie and Trena, thank you for putting me in check and keeping me grounded during the early days of Bludso's Compton. And to the rest of the staff, thank you for getting us off the ground and helping to make Bludso's more than a BBQ stand.

The OGs at Bludso's Hollywood, Jason, James, and Noah, thank you; and thank you to everyone since. But, especially, thank you for everything you did in 2020, for keeping us going and thriving during that time. So, Jimmy, Kevin, Tad, and the rest of the great staff – you know who you are – thank you.

The Bludso's restaurant family from Down Under, thank you. The Crown Casino in Melbourne, Australia, brought us down there and believed that our BBQ restaurant belonged on the other side of the world. Your hospitality was second to none.

Kingsford Charcoal, wow, I don't even have the words. Let me just say this, I love you all for understanding that sometimes the helper needs help.

Everyone at Ten Speed Press! Dervla Kelly and Emma Campion, thank you for having the confidence in me and my story and that you wanted to take the time to have me tell it. I really appreciate you guys. We are family now and I look forward to a long-lasting relationship. Thank you to Doug Ogan, Sohayla Farman, Mari Gill, Dan Myers, Jane Chinn, Janina Lawrence, Sharon Silva, Samantha Simon, and Natalie Yera for all the amazing work you do. People don't realize the amount of effort that goes into a cookbook, and you all are the ones who make that happen.

Alison Fargis, my incredible agent, thank you for being my voice. Thank you for letting me drive, but always knowing the direction I was heading. Thank you for all the introductions to new family and special people. Thank you for being amazing.

I want to thank all the Bludso's customers from near and far! From the Cpt to Australia – without you, none of this is possible.

Index

Library of Congress Cataloging-in-Publication Data
  Names: Bludso, Kevin, 1965- author. | Galuten, Noah, author.
  Title: Bludso's bbq cookbook : a family affair in smoke and soul /
    by Kevin Bludso with Noah Galuten.
  Description: California : Ten Speed Press, 2022. | Includes index.
  Identifiers: LCCN 2021021104 (print) | LCCN 2021021105 (ebook) |
    ISBN 9781984859556 (hardcover) | ISBN 9781984859563 (ebook)
  Subjects: LCSH: Barbecuing — Texas. | Restaurants — Texas.
  Classification: LCC TX840.B3 B559 2022 (print) | LCC TX840.B3 (ebook) |
    DDC 641.7/609764 — dc23
  LC record available at https://lccn.loc.gov/2021021104
  LC ebook record available at https://lccn.loc.gov/2021021105

Hardcover ISBN: 978-1-9848-5955-6
eBook ISBN: 978-1-9848-5956-3

Printed in China

Photographs on the front cover; back endpaper; pages vii, 2, 3, 5 (top),
  6, 9 (top right, middle, bottom left), 10, 11, 22, 28–29, 42, 61, 122, 142, 146,
  186–187, 205, 216, 262–263, 266, and 267 by Demetrius Smith. Photograph
  on page 121 by Rasheed Philips. (Copyright by Bludso's Bar & Que.)
Photographs on pages 5 (bottom right), 17, 18, and 21 by Regina Karon.
  (Copyright by Crown Melbourne.)
Photographs on pages 5 (bottom left), 9 (top left, middle left, middle right),
  15, 25, and 26–27 are courtesy of the Bludso Family.

Editor: Dervla Kelly | Production editors: Doug Ogan and Sohayla Farman
Designer: Emma Campion | Production designer: Mari Gill
Cover artist: Duke Aber
Typefaces: Linotype's Neue Haas Grotesk; Commercial Type's
  Publico Banner; Commercial Type's Publico Text; and Active Images'
  CCGothChicBlack Regular
Production manager: Dan Myers | Prepress color manager: Jane Chinn
Copyeditor: Sharon Silva | Proofreader: Janina Lawrence
Indexer: Ken DellaPenta
Publicist: Natalie Yera | Marketer: Samantha Simon

10 9 8 7 6 5 4 3 2 1

First Edition

Kevin Bludso is a chef, television personality, and two-time Steve Harvey Neighborhood Award winner. In 2008, he opened Bludso's BBQ in Compton, California, and it has since grown into an international empire, with a flagship restaurant, Bludso's Bar & Que, in Hollywood, a concession stand at the LAFC soccer stadium, a location in Proud Bird by LAX, and a sprawling restaurant and bar called San Antone by Bludso's BBQ in the Crown Casino in Melbourne, Australia. He is returning for a second season as a the star of Netflix's hit BBQ competition show *The American Barbecue Showdown*, and has multiple television appearances on shows such as *Diners, Drive-Ins and Dives* and *Bong Appétit*, and as a recurring guest judge on *Bar Rescue*. Kevin currently resides in Corsicana, Texas, regularly traveling both nationally and internationally for his pop-up events and television appearances.

Noah Galuten is a chef, restaurant consultant, and James Beard Award–nominated cookbook author. After working as a food writer, he trained in Compton under Kevin Bludso and became the chef of the ever-popular Bludso's Bar & Que in Los Angeles. Noah went on to work on the launches of beloved Los Angeles restaurants Cofax Coffee, Prime Pizza (now with four locations), and Yojimbo. He also co-authored Phaidon's *On Vegetables: Modern Recipes for the Home Kitchen* with Jeremy Fox— and his debut solo cookbook, *The Don't Panic Pantry Cookbook*, is coming out in the fall of 2022 for Knopf.

Eric Wolfinger is a James Beard Award–winning photographer whose idea of a good time always involves fire and food. When not shooting photos, he works as a short-order cook for his partner and their two kids in San Diego.

Demetrius Smith is a wedding, portrait, sports, and event photographer who lives in the West Valley of Arizona. He is inspired by his beautiful wife, Aunjel Smith, from both sides of the lens.

THE
BLUDSO
FAMILY